# Contents

# Introduction

Learning to read is *the* goal for all students, but unfortunately success is not a given. Many students, for many reasons, find reading an enormous challenge. Despite excellent reading programs, dedicated teachers, and various kinds of interventions, far too many students emerge from the primary grades as struggling readers. One way in which to help these students is through additional phonics instruction.

While phonics instruction is an important tool for all readers, it is particularly necessary for those who are at risk for learning difficulties because of poor reading skills. A phonics background—understanding the relationship between sounds and spellings—enables a reader to decode with ease. Decoding aids in word recognition. When students can identify words quickly and accurately, their reading fluency improves. When students spend less time struggling with decoding, their reading comprehension improves.

By offering opportunities to review or learn anew basic phonics principles, the lessons in this book help students develop and reinforce decoding skills. You can use the lessons in the sequence given or choose those needed to address specific weaknesses in a student's phonics background.

## Lesson Organization

Each lesson is three pages long and addresses a particular phonics principle.

*The first lesson page includes:*

- a statement of the phonics principle for the lesson

- examples of the phonics principle

- a simple activity reinforcing the principle

- one or two other exercises

*The second page includes:*

- three exercises, including rhyming, word meaning, synonyms, antonyms, homophones, or extending the phonics principle

**■SCHOLASTIC**

Grades 3–6

# EXTRA PRACTICE FOR
# *Struggling Readers*

## PHONICS

**Linda Ward Beech**

New York • Toronto • London • Auckland • Sydney
Mexico City • New Delhi • Hong Kong • Buenos Aires

**Teaching** *Resources*

Editor: Mela Ottaiano
Cover design: Brian LaRossa
Interior design: Melinda Belter
Interior illustrations: Teresa Anderko

ISBN-13: 978-0-545-12409-6
ISBN-10: 0-545-12409-3

22 23        40        22  21  20

*The third page includes:*

- two word-meaning exercises including puzzles or riddles

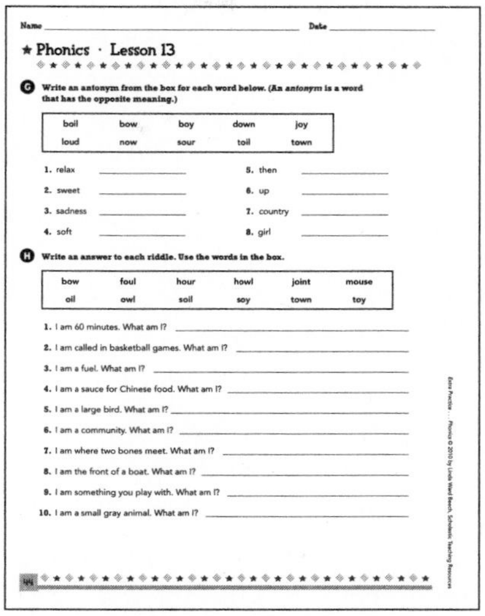

Name ____________ Date ____________

★ Phonics · Lesson 13

**G** **Write an antonym from the box for each word below. (An *antonym* is a word that has the opposite meaning.)**

| | | | | |
|---|---|---|---|---|
| boil | bow | boy | down | joy |
| loud | now | sour | toil | town |

1. relax ____________
2. sweet ____________
3. sadness ____________
4. soft ____________
5. then ____________
6. up ____________
7. country ____________
8. girl ____________

**H** **Write an answer to each riddle. Use the words in the box.**

| | | | | | |
|---|---|---|---|---|---|
| bow | foul | hour | howl | joint | mouse |
| oil | owl | soil | soy | town | toy |

1. I am 60 minutes. What am I? ____________
2. I am called in basketball games. What am I? ____________
3. I am a fuel. What am I? ____________
4. I am a sauce for Chinese food. What am I? ____________
5. I am a large bird. What am I? ____________
6. I am a community. What am I? ____________
7. I am where two bones meet. What am I? ____________
8. I am the front of a boat. What am I? ____________
9. I am something you play with. What am I? ____________
10. I am a small gray animal. What am I? ____________

Extra Practice . . . Phonics © 2010 by Linda Ward Beech, Scholastic Teaching Resources

44

## Ways to Make the Most of the Lessons

- Before introducing these lessons, be sure that students have alphabetical recognition and some phonemic awareness.
- Use the lessons in the classroom for extra practice during regular reading time or as individual assignments. Send the lessons home for students to do as homework or to complete with an adult.
- Some lessons have Phonics Alerts that point out variations on a particular phonics principle. When students find exceptions to a principle, explain that these principles are generalizations that usually apply, but not always.
- Review, review, review. For example, when students are working on a lesson about initial blends, they will also encounter various vowel sounds. Take a minute to remind students about what they already know about those vowel sounds. Help students focus on *all* the letters or spellings in a word.
- Reinforce a phonics focus by having students create their own word webs for words illustrating different principles, such as blends, long and short vowels, digraphs, and so on.
- Use the lessons to expand students' vocabulary. Words that exemplify a phonics principle are not always familiar to students. Some examples: *bog, jag, sly, reek, hue*. Keep dictionaries handy for when students encounter these words.
- An understanding of phonics can improve spelling. Create spelling lists using the different principles covered in the lessons.
- Create word lists from each lesson. Students can use them to practice blending, in word sorts, on word walls, in writing assignments, or in reader's journals.
- Some lessons require students to write tongue twisters. Challenge students to make up the longest tongue twister, the funniest one, or the one that is the most difficult to say. Then hold a contest to see who can say the twister the fastest or the most clearly.
- Build on lessons with riddle games. For example: *What starts with /s/ and rhymes with dip?* After introducing a few examples, encourage students to write their own riddles for classmates to solve.
- Keep observation charts to monitor progress.

# ★ Phonics · Lesson 1

## Consonants and Short Vowels

If a word has one vowel between two consonants, the vowel usually has a short sound.

Consonants:   **B   D   G   L   M   N   P   S   T   X**

Short Vowels:

A in **bat**     E in **net**     I in **pig**     O in **mop**     U in **sun**

**A**   Say the name of each picture. Write the correct vowel to complete the word.

1.  t ___ p     2.  **10**  t ___ n     3.  b ___ b     4.  b ___ d     5.  p ___ n

6.  p ___ p     7.  l ___ g     8.  ___ x     9.  t ___ b     10.  m ___ p

**B**   Add the vowel to make new words. Read the words.

| Add a | Add e | Add i | Add o | Add u |
|-------|-------|-------|-------|-------|
| t ___ p | p ___ n | t ___ p | b ___ b | b ___ b |
| t ___ n | p ___ p | t ___ n | p ___ p | b ___ d |
| b ___ d |  | b ___ d | l ___ g | p ___ n |
| p ___ n |  | p ___ p | ___ x | l ___ g |
| l ___ g |  |  | m ___ p |  |
| t ___ b |  |  |  |  |

# ★ Phonics · Lesson 1

**C** **Read the words in the box. Write the words with short /a/ and /e/.**

| beg | dug | ban | dog | den | dam |
|-----|-----|-----|-----|-----|-----|
| gas | nut | box | nag | let | gem |

**Short /a/** _____ _____ _____ _____

**Short /e/** _____ _____ _____ _____

> **PHONICS ALERT!**
>
> The consonants c and g have two sounds:
>
> /k/ in **cat**
> /s/ in **cent**
> /g/ in **get**
> /j/ in **gem**

**D** **Read the words in the box. Write the words with short /i/, /o/, and /u/.**

| pig | got | gum | pep | not | tax |
|-----|-----|-----|-----|-----|-----|
| sis | lip | mud | tug | bog | met |

**Short /i/** _____ _____ _____

**Short /o/** _____ _____ _____

**Short /u/** _____ _____ _____

**E** **Write a word from the box to rhyme with each underlined word.**

| lot | net | pig | bag | men | lad |
|-----|-----|-----|-----|-----|-----|
| bin | but | Pop | nap | man | us |

1. A <u>tag</u> on the _____
2. <u>Ten</u> _____
3. A <u>big</u> _____
4. A <u>mad</u> _____
5. <u>Get</u> the _____

6. <u>In</u> the _____
7. A <u>bus</u> for _____
8. A <u>tan</u> _____
9. A <u>mop</u> for _____
10. <u>Not</u> a _____

# ★ Phonics · Lesson 1

**F** Write a synonym from the box for each word below. (A *synonym* is a word that has a similar meaning.)

| unhappy | insect | sack | bright | top | talk |
|---------|--------|------|--------|-----|------|
| father | small | dark | mother | family | large |

**1.** lid _____

**2.** dad _____

**3.** sad _____

**4.** big _____

**5.** dim _____

**6.** bug _____

**7.** mom _____

**8.** bag _____

**9.** gab _____

**G** Write an answer to each riddle. Use the words in the box.

| tug | ten | bat | pen | bun |
|-----|-----|-----|-----|-----|
| mug | nip | dig | sun | pug |

**1.** I have wings. What am I? _____

**2.** I can write. What am I? _____

**3.** I am good to eat. What am I? _____

**4.** I am a dog. What am I? _____

**5.** I am a boat. What am I? _____

**6.** I am hot. What am I? _____

**7.** I am a number. What am I? _____

**8.** I am like a cup. What am I? _____

# ★ Phonics · Lesson 2

## More Consonants and Short Vowels

If a word has one vowel between two consonants, the vowel usually has a short sound.

Consonants:  C  F  H  J  K  R  V  W  Y  Z

Short Vowels:

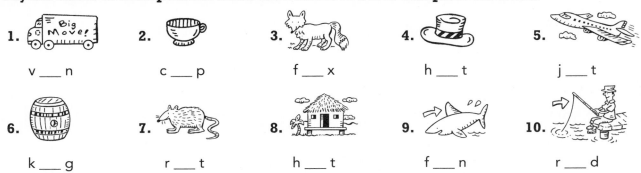

A in        E in        I in        O in        U in

fan         hen         wig         cot         rug

**A**  Say the name of each picture. Write the correct vowel to complete the word.

1. v ___ n

2. c ___ p

3. f ___ x

4. h ___ t

5. j ___ t

6. k ___ g

7. r ___ t

8. h ___ t

9. f ___ n

10. r ___ d

**B**  Read the words in the box. Listen for the short vowel sound.
Write each word in the correct column on the chart.

| | | | | |
|---|---|---|---|---|
| fed | rid | rut | fat | cog |
| jug | had | hug | rap | ram |
| kit | jot | fun | zip | yes |
| cod | hot | yip | wet | hem |

| Short a | Short e | Short i | Short o | Short u |
|---|---|---|---|---|
| _____ | _____ | _____ | _____ | _____ |
| _____ | _____ | _____ | _____ | _____ |
| _____ | _____ | _____ | _____ | _____ |
| _____ | _____ | _____ | _____ | _____ |

# ★ Phonics · Lesson 2

**C** **Write a word from the box to rhyme with each underlined word.**

| | | | |
|---|---|---|---|
| rug | jag | yam | hog |
| cat | ran | fox | hot |
| vet | wig | hum | fun |

**PHONICS ALERT!**

The letter y can be a consonant or a vowel:

consonant: **yet**

short /i/: **gym**

**1.** A fat _____

**2.** The man _____ .

**3.** A _____ in a box

**4.** Have _____ in the sun .

**5.** A _____ pot

**6.** A _____ on a log

**7.** Get the _____ .

**8.** A big _____

**9.** A bug on a _____

**10.** Ham and a _____

**D** **Circle the word that makes sense in the sentence.**

**1.** Jim can ____ the pot.                fox        fix

**2.** Bud has on a red ____ .            cap        cup

**3.** Did Jan ____ a lot?                jug        jog

**4.** Kit fed the ____ .                    ran        ram

**5.** Rod had ____ on his lip.          jag        jam

**6.** Did Mom rip the ____ ?           hem        hum

**7.** Jen had the pup on her ____ .  lap        lop

**8.** The cat hid in the ____ .          hit        hat

**9.** The rim of the ____ is wet.      cup        cop

**10.** Meg and Ken had ____ .          fin        fun

# ★ Phonics · Lesson 2

**E** Write a synonym from the box for each word below. (A *synonym* is a word that has a similar meaning.)

| wave | run | tear | wit | hat | gag |
|------|-----|------|-----|-----|-----|
| barrel | smack | zig | chubby | pitcher | vigor |

**1.** jog _____

**2.** keg _____

**3.** rip _____

**4.** cap _____

**5.** fat _____

**6.** hit _____

**7.** vim _____

**8.** jug _____

**9.** wag _____

**F** Write an answer to each riddle. Use the words in the box.

| fog | fax | cud | vet | cod |
|-----|-----|-----|-----|-----|
| fig | hen | jet | vat | wax |

**1.** I am a fish. What am I? _____

**2.** I am a fruit. What am I? _____

**3.** I am what a cow chews. What am I? _____

**4.** I am an animal doctor. What am I? _____

**5.** I lay eggs. What am I? _____

**6.** I make floors shine. What am I? _____

**7.** I am a plane. What am I? _____

**8.** I am thick and gray. What am I? _____

# ★ Phonics · Lesson 3

## Long Vowel CVCe Words With A

Words with the long /ā/ sound often end in *silent e*.

| C | A | K | E |
|---|---|---|---|
| consonant | vowel | consonant | silent e |

**A** Read each pair of words. Write the word with the long /ā/ vowel sound.

1. tape   tap   _____

2. pan   pane   _____

3. mat   mate   _____

4. vane   van   _____

5. mad   made   _____

6. gap   gape   _____

7. rage   rag   _____

8. fad   fade   _____

9. fate   fat   _____

10. dame   dam   _____

**B** Underline each word with a long /ā/ sound. Write the word.

1. bag   _____

2. face   _____

3. rake   _____

4. mane   _____

5. can   _____

6. cave   _____

7. take   _____

8. lane   _____

9. hat   _____

**C** Write the correct word for each picture.

1.

ran   rake

_____

2.

gate   gab

_____

3.

map   maze

_____

# ★ Phonics · Lesson 3

★◆★◆★◆★◆★◆★◆★◆★◆★◆★◆★◆★◆★◆★◆★◆★◆★◆

**D** **Write a word from the box to rhyme with each underlined word.**

| game | wave | male | late | cake |
|------|------|------|------|------|
| tap | race | pane | haze | man |

**1.** I <u>hate</u> to be _____ .

**2.** The <u>same</u> _____

**3.** The <u>pace</u> of the _____

**4.** A <u>gaze</u> in the _____

**5.** <u>Bake</u> a _____ .

**6.** I <u>gave</u> a _____ .

**7.** A <u>pale</u> _____

**8.** The <u>cane</u> hit the _____ .

**E** **Write three words that rhyme with each word below.**

**1.** sane        **2.** daze        **3.** wage

_____   _____   _____

_____   _____   _____

_____   _____   _____

**F** **Write a long /ā/ word from the box in each shape.**

| vine | mope | wade | rage | gave |
|------|------|------|------|------|
| gape | fake | lace | ate | maze |

**1.**

**2.**

**3.**

**4.**

**5.**

**6.**

**7.**

**8.**

# ★ Phonics · Lesson 3

**G** Write an antonym from the box for each word below. (An *antonym* is a word that has the opposite meaning.)

| love | real | female | give | wild |
|------|------|--------|------|------|
| alike | early | keep | lose | different |

**1.** late _____

**2.** fake _____

**3.** male _____

**4.** take _____

**5.** same _____

**6.** save _____

**7.** tame _____

**8.** hate _____

**H** Write an answer to each riddle. Use the words in the box.

| vase | game | vane | wave | sale |
|------|------|------|------|------|
| mane | tame | cake | rake | pane |

**1.** I am something you play. What am I? _____

**2.** I am in the sea. What am I? _____

**3.** I hold flowers. What am I? _____

**4.** I am good to eat. What am I? _____

**5.** I am part of a horse. What am I? _____

**6.** I am a garden tool. What am I? _____

**7.** I am on a roof. What am I? _____

**8.** I am part of a window. What am I? _____

# ★ Phonics · Lesson 4

### More Spellings for Long A

Long /ā/ can be spelled *ai* or *ay*.

pail                    hay

**A**  Read each pair of words. Write the word with the long /ā/ vowel sound.

1. pad   paid   _____

2. bait   bat   _____

3. gab   gay   _____

4. aid   and   _____

5. may   map   _____

6. had   hail   _____

7. ray   rag   _____

8. fail   fat   _____

9. sag   say   _____

10. bay   ban   _____

**B**  Underline each word with the long /ā/ sound. Write the word.

1. wait   _____

2. ray   _____

3. rat   _____

4. wail   _____

5. gas   _____

6. tag   _____

7. bad   _____

8. raid   _____

9. bay   _____

**C**  Write the correct word for each picture.

1.

sail   sale

_____

2.

vain   vane

_____

3.

tale   tail

_____

# ★ Phonics · Lesson 4

**D** **Write a word from the box to rhyme with each underlined word.**

| hail | bay | wait | rage |
|------|-----|------|------|
| maid | pane | pave | game |

1. I <u>paid</u> the _____ .

2. Can you <u>sail</u> in the _____ ?

3. <u>Rain</u> on the _____

4. If you _____ , you'll be <u>late</u>.

5. The <u>way</u> to the _____

6. The <u>aim</u> of the _____

**E** **Write a synonym from the box for each word below. (A *synonym* is a word that has a similar meaning.)**

| cry | prison | speak | race |
|-----|--------|-------|------|
| pause | make | help | hurt |

1. say _____

2. aid _____

3. wait _____

4. maim _____

5. wail _____

6. jail _____

**F** **Circle the word that makes sense in the sentence.**

1. Did Ray ____ to pay the man?         **fate**      **fail**      **fade**

2. May ____ on the bed.                  **lay**       **lake**      **lace**

3. Did Jane ____ into the bay?           **sale**      **same**      **sail**

4. Wade gave ____ to the cat.            **ate**       **aid**       **ail**

5. Gail will wait for the ____ .         **main**      **made**      **mail**

6. Will it ____ on the day of the game?  **rake**      **rain**      **rail**

7. Jay has a ____ at the base of his nail. **pain**    **pail**      **page**

8. Dale had to wait to get ____ .        **pale**      **pace**      **paid**

# ★ Phonics · Lesson 4

**G** Write a long /ā/ word from the box in each shape.

| win | vain | bail | dot | jail |
|-----|------|------|-----|------|
| day | mail | way | gay | gain |

1. 

2. 

3. 

4. 

5. 

6. 

7. 

8. 

**H** Write an answer to each riddle. Use the words in the box.

| tail | jay | bait | pay | May |
|------|-----|------|-----|-----|
| rain | maid | mail | pail | rail |

**1.** I am wet. What am I? _____

**2.** I can wag. What am I? _____

**3.** I am a month. What am I? _____

**4.** I help catch fish. What am I? _____

**5.** I hold things. What am I? _____

**6.** I need a stamp. What am I? _____

**7.** I work in a hotel. What am I? _____

**8.** I am a bird. What am I? _____

# ★ Phonics · Lesson 5

## Long Vowel CVCe Words With I

Words with the long /ī/ sound often end in *silent e*.

| D | I | M | E |
|---|---|---|---|
| consonant | vowel | consonant | silent e |

**A** Read each pair of words. Write the word with the long /ī/ vowel sound.

1. din  dine  _____

2. hid  hide  _____

3. kite  kit  _____

4. pin  pine  _____

5. dime  dim  _____

6. ride  rid  _____

7. site  sit  _____

8. fine  fin  _____

9. rip  ripe  _____

10. bit  bite  _____

**B** Underline each word with the long /ī/ sound. Write the word.

1. lice  _____

2. pike  _____

3. rig  _____

4. sip  _____

5. mime  _____

6. rite  _____

7. like  _____

8. vile  _____

9. did  _____

**C** Write the correct word for each picture.

1. hive  hit

_____

2. big  bike

_____

3. pit  pipe

_____

# ★ Phonics · Lesson 5

★ ◆ ★ ◆ ★ ◆ ★ ◆ ★ ◆ ★ ◆ ★ ◆ ★ ◆ ★ ◆ ★ ◆ ★ ◆ ★ ◆ ★ ◆ ★ ◆ ★ ◆ ◆

**D**  Read the words in the box. Write the words with long /ī/ and long /ā/.

| vice | it | tame | aim | rite | bag |
|------|------|------|------|------|------|
| raid | wipe | fife | lay | pit | tide |
| gape | tin | gab | pike | mate | sip |

**PHONICS**
**ALERT!**
⬇

The letter *i* can have a long vowel sound or a short vowel sound in some CVCe words:

Short /i/ in **give** and **live**

Long /ī/ in **hive** and **live**

**Long /ī/**

_____  _____

_____  _____

_____  _____

**Long /ā/**

_____  _____

_____  _____

_____  _____

**E**  Write a word from the box to rhyme with each underlined word.

| sis | tide | site | tile | rise | lip |
|------|------|------|------|------|------|
| pipe | nine | bike | five | nice | life |

**1.** I <u>dine</u> at _____ .

**2.** The <u>rice</u> is _____ .

**3.** A <u>wife</u> for _____

**4.** I <u>like</u> to _____ .

**5.** Mike was <u>wise</u> to _____ .

**6.** <u>Wipe</u> the _____ .

**7.** A <u>kite</u> on the _____

**8.** I <u>ride</u> the _____ .

**9.** A <u>pile</u> of _____

**10.** Let's <u>dive</u> at _____ .

**F**  Write three rhyming words for each word below.

**1.** line    _____    _____    _____

**2.** hide    _____    _____    _____

**3.** bike    _____    _____    _____

# ★ Phonics · Lesson 5

**G** Write an antonym from the box for each word below. (An *antonym* is a word that has the opposite meaning.)

| dead | unwise | virtue | thick | mean | narrow |
|------|--------|--------|-------|------|--------|
| man | dislike | fall | unripe | yours | husband |

1. nice _____

2. like _____

3. ripe _____

4. wife _____

5. wise _____

6. wide _____

7. rise _____

8. vice _____

9. live _____

10. mine _____

**H** Write an answer to each riddle. Use the words in the box.

| vine | pine | dice | dime | vile |
|------|------|------|------|------|
| kite | fife | lime | five | bike |

1. I am used in games. What am I? _____

2. I am played in bands. What am I? _____

3. I have two wheels. What am I? _____

4. I fly in the sky. What am I? _____

5. I am a number less than six. What am I? _____

6. I am a green fruit. What am I? _____

7. I am a coin. What am I? _____

8. I am a tree. What am I? _____

# ★ Phonics · Lesson 6

---

## More Spellings for Long I

Long /ī/ can be spelled *igh*, *y*, or *ye*.

fight          my          bye

---

**A**  **Read each pair of words. Write the word with the long /ī/ sound.**

1. bit   bye        _____        6. fry   fig        _____

2. tight   tin      _____        7. right   rim      _____

3. dip   dry        _____        8. sigh   sin       _____

4. his   high       _____        9. rip   rye        _____

5. by   big         _____       10. lip   light      _____

**B**  **Circle all the words in the box that have a long /ī/ vowel sound.**

| | | | | |
|---|---|---|---|---|
| pile | nip | rid | night | rice |
| vim | dry | why | bite | light |
| bye | kin | my | tip | high |
| time | spy | jig | fry | wise |

**C**  **Write the correct word for each picture.**

1.

cry   try

_____

2.

sight   sigh

_____

3.

tile   tights

_____

# ★ Phonics · Lesson 6

**D** **Write a word from the box to complete each sentence.**

| Why | my | fly | try | cry | dry | by | sky |
|-----|-----|-----|-----|-----|-----|-----|-----|

**1.** I will take _____ dog, Ike, for a walk.

**2.** Ike is _____ the door.

**3.** The _____ looks dark. Will it rain?

**4.** Ike starts to _____ .

**5.** He does not _____ out the door for his walk.

**6.** I _____ to make Ike go out.

**7.** Ike wants to stay _____ .

**8.** _____ does it have to rain now?

**E** **Using the words in the box, write an antonym (An *antonym* is a word that has the opposite meaning) with a long / ī / vowel sound for each word below.**

| shy | high | light | fight | sky |
|-----|------|-------|-------|-----|
| tight | fly | night | dry | bye |

**1.** hi _____

**2.** dark _____

**3.** day _____

**4.** loose _____

**5.** earth _____

**6.** wet _____

**7.** bold _____

**8.** low _____

**F** **Write a sentence of your own using each of these words.**

**1.** fry _____

**2.** might _____

# ★ Phonics · Lesson 6

**G**  **Draw a line from the picture to each word that rhymes with *eye*.**

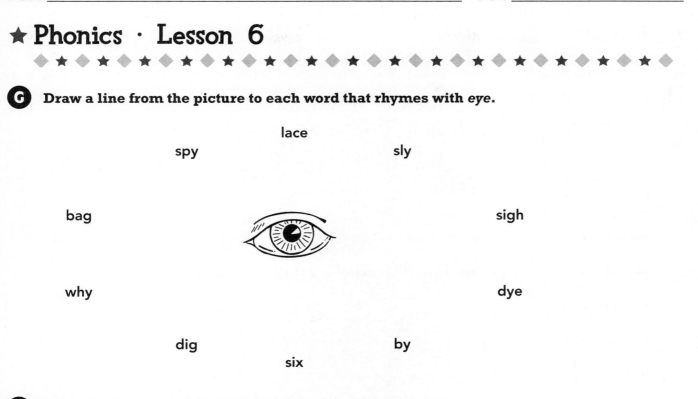

lace

spy                    sly

bag                                        sigh

why                                        dye

dig                          by

six

**H**  **Write an answer to each riddle. Use the words from the box.**

| tight | sky | dye | rye | fight |
|-------|-----|-----|-----|-------|
| night | spy | right | cry | sight |

**1.** I add color to things. What am I? _____

**2.** I am where planes fly. What am I? _____

**3.** I am one of your senses. What am I? _____

**4.** I am a grain used in bread. What am I? _____

**5.** I am the time when you sleep. What am I? _____

**6.** I am a direction. What am I? _____

**7.** I am sneaky. What am I? _____

**8.** I am what boxers do. What am I? _____

# ★ Phonics · Lesson 7

## Long Vowel Spellings With E

Long /ē/ can be spelled *e* or *ee*.

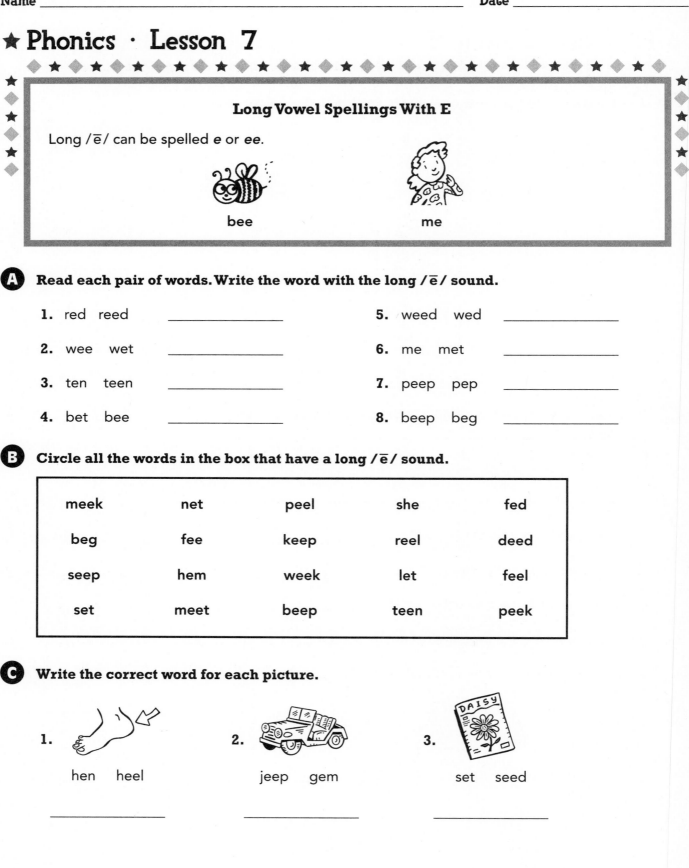

bee

me

**A**  **Read each pair of words. Write the word with the long /ē/ sound.**

1. red  reed  _____
2. wee  wet  _____
3. ten  teen  _____
4. bet  bee  _____
5. weed  wed  _____
6. me  met  _____
7. peep  pep  _____
8. beep  beg  _____

**B**  **Circle all the words in the box that have a long /ē/ sound.**

| | | | | |
|---|---|---|---|---|
| meek | net | peel | she | fed |
| beg | fee | keep | reel | deed |
| seep | hem | week | let | feel |
| set | meet | beep | teen | peek |

**C**  **Write the correct word for each picture.**

1. hen  heel

_____

2. jeep  gem

_____

3. set  seed

_____

# ★ Phonics · Lesson 7

★◆★◆★◆★◆★◆★◆★◆★◆★◆★◆★◆★◆★◆★◆★◆★◆

**D** **Write a word from the box to complete each sentence.**

| | | | |
|---|---|---|---|
| beep | jeep | deep | veep |
| keep | weep | seep | peep |

1. Dee is a vice president, or _____ , at her job.

2. She drives to work in a _____ .

3. She gives a _____ of her horn when she leaves.

4. This week there was a _____ hole in the road.

5. Dee could not _____ out of the hole.

6. She got out to _____ at the jeep in the hole.

7. She saw oil _____ out of the jeep.

8. It made Dee want to _____ .

**E** **Circle the word that makes sense in the sentence.**

| | | | |
|---|---|---|---|
| 1. Have you ____ Lee? | seem | seen | see |
| 2. She paid the ____ for the ride. | feel | feed | fee |
| 3. Vee gave me a box to ____ . | keg | keel | keep |
| 4. Will he ____ a reel to fish? | need | net | meek |
| 5. My ____ got wet in the rain. | fed | fate | feet |
| 6. Can we ____ by the bay? | met | make | meet |
| 7. Dale will ____ fine in a week. | be | bee | beep |
| 8. Did Miles ____ the red jeep? | seep | see | seed |

# ★ Phonics · Lesson 7

**F** Circle six words in the puzzle that rhyme with *heed*. Circle four words in the puzzle that rhyme with *week*. Then write the words on the lines.

| | | | | | | | | |
|---|---|---|---|---|---|---|---|---|
| L | E | E | K | A | Y | P | G | K |
| B | W | I | M | R | E | E | D | A |
| Z | E | D | O | E | F | E | E | D |
| M | E | E | K | E | S | K | X | J |
| F | D | E | J | K | V | H | N | Q |
| L | H | D | N | T | R | M | E | E |
| P | T | B | L | I | O | F | E | C |
| U | D | G | N | S | E | E | D | W |

**heed** _____  _____

_____  _____

_____  _____

**week** _____  _____

_____  _____

**G** Write an answer to each riddle. Use the words in the box.

| | | | | |
|---|---|---|---|---|
| weed | be | week | teen | beet |
| peep | reef | tee | eel | bee |

**1.** I am a sound a baby bird makes. What am I? _____

**2.** I live in water and look like a snake. What am I? _____

**3.** I grow where I am not wanted. What am I? _____

**4.** I make honey. What am I? _____

**5.** I am seven days. What am I? _____

**6.** I am used in golf. What am I? _____

**7.** I am between ages 13 and 19. What am I? _____

**8.** I am red and good to eat. What am I? _____

# ★ Phonics · Lesson 8

### More Spellings for Long E

Long /ē/ can be spelled **ea** and **y**.

seal                    bunny

**A**    **Read each pair of words. Write the word with the long /ē/ sound.**

1. red   read    _____
2. lead   led    _____
3. set   seat    _____
4. neat   net    _____

5. beat   bet    _____
6. met   meat    _____
7. pet   peat    _____
8. bead   bed    _____

**B**    **Underline each word with a long /ē/ sound. Write the word.**

1. deal    _____
2. neat    _____
3. beg    _____
4. keep    _____
5. pep    _____
6. we    _____

7. kitty    _____
8. men    _____
9. heap    _____
10. sea    _____
11. be    _____
12. funny    _____

**C**    **Write the correct word for each picture.**

1.    bean   beam

2.    tee   tea

3.    lap   leap

_____    _____    _____

# ★ Phonics · Lesson 8

**D** Draw a line from the picture to each word that rhymes with *beak.*

led

leek                                    seek

keg                                                        peak

meek                                                              wed

reek                                              week

leak                      peek

**E** Circle the correct homophone for each word meaning. (A *homophone* is a word that sounds like another word but has a different meaning and a different spelling.)

| | | | |
|---|---|---|---|
| **1.** | food that comes from an animal | **meet** | **meat** |
| **2.** | not strong | **weak** | **week** |
| **3.** | part of a foot | **heal** | **heel** |
| **4.** | a group of players who work together | **teem** | **team** |
| **5.** | the opposite of fake | **real** | **reel** |
| **6.** | what bells do when they ring | **peel** | **peal** |
| **7.** | something to drink | **tee** | **tea** |
| **8.** | the top of a mountain | **peak** | **peek** |
| **9.** | what a pipe might do | **leek** | **leak** |
| **10.** | where fish are found | **sea** | **see** |

# ★ Phonics · Lesson 8

★◆★◆★◆★◆★◆★◆★◆★◆★◆★◆★◆★◆★◆★◆★◆

**F**  **Read the clues. Then fill in the puzzle with five long /ē/ words, one long /ā/ word and one long /ī/ word.**

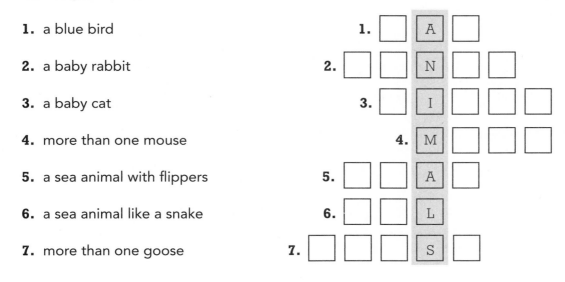

1. a blue bird

2. a baby rabbit

3. a baby cat

4. more than one mouse

5. a sea animal with flippers

6. a sea animal like a snake

7. more than one goose

**G**  **Write an answer to each riddle. Use the words in the box.**

| seat | city | lean | leaf | beef | baby |
|------|------|------|------|------|------|
| pea | heat | taffy | seam | heap | meal |

1. I am what you eat three times a day. What am I? _____

2. I grow on a tree. What am I? _____

3. I am a pile of things. What am I? _____

4. I am a young child. What am I? _____

5. I am a kind of candy. What am I? _____

6. I grow in a pod. What am I? _____

7. I have big buildings and lots of people. What am I? _____

8. I am what you sit on. What am I? _____

9. I come from the sun. What am I? _____

10. I am something you sew. What am I? _____

# ★ Phonics · Lesson 9

## Long Vowel CVCe Words With O

Words with the long /ō/ sounds often end in *silent e*.

| H | O | L | E |
|---|---|---|---|
| consonant | vowel | consonant | silent e |

**A** **Read each pair of words. Write the word with the long /ō/ sound.**

1. code   cod   _____

2. not   note   _____

3. mop   mope   _____

4. rod   rode   _____

5. lob   lobe   _____

6. hop   hope   _____

7. pope   pop   _____

8. rote   rot   _____

**B** **Change the first vowel in each word to make a long /ō/ word.**

1. cape   ➡   c ___ pe

2. pile   ➡   p ___ le

3. pipe   ➡   p ___ pe

4. rate   ➡   r ___ te

5. mile   ➡   m ___ le

6. cave   ➡   c ___ ve

7. wake   ➡   w ___ ke

8. line   ➡   l ___ ne

9. ripe   ➡   r ___ pe

10. dame   ➡   d ___ me

**C** **Write the correct word for each picture.**

1.

rob   robe

_____

2.

nose   nice

_____

3.

bane   bone

_____

# ★ Phonics · Lesson 9

**D**  **Write a word from the box to rhyme with each underlined word.**

| | | | | |
|---|---|---|---|---|
| code | vote | hole | cove | dome |
| poke | lox | rose | cog | cope |

**1.** I <u>hope</u> to _____ .

**2.** A <u>home</u> with a _____

**3.** He <u>dove</u> in the _____ .

**4.** Did you <u>note</u> the _____ ?

**5.** A <u>mole</u> in a _____

**6.** A <u>hose</u> on a _____

**7.** What <u>mode</u> is the _____ ?

**8.** She <u>woke</u> him with a _____ .

**E**  **Write four words that rhyme with each word below.**

**1.** tone

**2.** role

**3.** hope

_____     _____     _____

_____     _____     _____

_____     _____     _____

_____     _____     _____

**F**  **Each word below is in the past tense. Write the present tense of the word.**

**1.** wove          _____

**2.** rode          _____

**3.** woke          _____

**4.** dove          _____

# ★ Phonics · Lesson 9

◆ ★ ◆ ★ ◆ ★ ◆ ★ ◆ ★ ◆ ★ ◆ ★ ◆ ★ ◆ ★ ◆ ★ ◆ ★ ◆ ★ ◆ ★ ◆ ★ ◆ ★ ◆ ★ ◆

**G** Write a synonym from the box for each word below. (A *synonym* is a word that has a similar meaning.)

| want | single | no | opening | sulk |
|------|--------|------|---------|------|
| part | rode | jab | area | elect |

**1.** mope _____

**2.** poke _____

**3.** vote _____

**4.** hope _____

**5.** hole _____

**6.** zone _____

**7.** lone _____

**8.** role _____

**H** Write an answer to each riddle. Use the words from the box.

| cone | rope | lobe | home | note |
|------|------|------|------|------|
| sole | pose | dome | hose | mode |

**1.** I am something that ties things together. What am I? _____

**2.** I am something you write. What am I? _____

**3.** I am where you live. What am I? _____

**4.** I can water a garden. What am I? _____

**5.** I am part of your foot. What am I? _____

**6.** I am round on top. What am I? _____

**7.** I am good with ice cream. What am I? _____

**8.** I am part of your ear. What am I? _____

# ★ Phonics · Lesson 10

## More Spellings for Long O

Long /ō/ can be spelled *o*, *oe*, *oa*, and *ow*.

toe          foam          bow

**Ⓐ** **Circle all the words in the box that have a long /ō/ sound.**

| go | tow | doe | fox | roam |
|------|------|------|------|------|
| load | tot | boat | yoke | moan |
| coal | dole | owe | goat | box |
| bop | hoe | foam | nod | mom |

**Ⓑ** **Change the vowel pairs in each word to make a long /ō/ word.**

1. lean  ➔  l __ __ n

2. bait  ➔  b __ __ t

3. fail  ➔  f __ __ l

4. mean  ➔  m __ __ n

5. raid  ➔  r __ __ d

6. meet  ➔  m __ __ t

7. gait  ➔  g __ __ t

8. seep  ➔  s __ __ p

9. seek  ➔  s __ __ k

10. bail  ➔  b __ __ l

**Ⓒ** **Write the correct word for each picture.**

1.    foal    feel

_____

2.    rug    row

_____

3.    got    goat

_____

# ★ Phonics · Lesson 10

**D** **Circle the word that makes sense in the sentence.**

| | | | | |
|---|---|---|---|---|
| 1. Did Joan ____ in the tub? | sub | soak | sail |
| 2. Joe went home, ____ I did too. | go | no | so |
| 3. The jet was ____ in the sky. | lot | log | low |
| 4. We will ____ in the mall. | rice | roam | row |
| 5. This is my ____ robe. | own | oat | oak |
| 6. Dad will ____ the grass. | woe | mow | mole |
| 7. A ____ is not a pal. | foe | fee | foal |
| 8. We will ____ to the cove for a dip. | got | sow | go |

**E** **Circle the correct homophone for each word meaning. (A *homophone* sounds like another word but has a different meaning and a different spelling.)**

| | | |
|---|---|---|
| 1. a street | rode | road |
| 2. to pull | tow | toe |
| 3. to lend something | lone | loan |
| 4. something that is carried | load | lode |
| 5. a garden tool | ho | hoe |

**F** **Write a sentence of your own using each of these words.**

1. toad _____

2. low _____

3. boat _____

# ★ Phonics · Lesson 10

**G** Draw a line from the picture to each word that rhymes with *doe.*

oat      row

so                    foe

not                   low

toe                   gob

woe           mow

no

**H** Write an answer to each riddle. Use the words from the box.

| | | | | | |
|---|---|---|---|---|---|
| loaf | soap | load | bowl | moat | oak |
| moan | boat | coal | goal | bow | coat |

**1.** I am used to heat homes. What am I? _____

**2.** I am tied with a ribbon. What am I? _____

**3.** I am a kind of dish. What am I? _____

**4.** I am used in a sink or tub. What am I? _____

**5.** I am scored in a hockey game. What am I? _____

**6.** I surround a castle. What am I? _____

**7.** I am something to wear when it's cold. What am I? _____

**8.** I am a kind of tree. What am I? _____

**9.** I am the form bread is in. What am I? _____

**10.** I am a low cry of pain. What am I? _____

# ★ Phonics · Lesson 11

## Long Vowel Spellings With U

Words with the long /ū/ sound often end in silent **e**.

Long /ū/ can also be spelled **ue**.

| M | U | L | E |
|---|---|---|---|
| consonant | vowel | consonant | silent e |

**A** Read each pair of words. Write the word with the long /ū/ sound.

1. dude   dud   _____

2. us   use   _____

3. jute   jut   _____

4. fuse   fuss   _____

5. cub   cube   _____

6. cut   cute   _____

**B** Circle all the words in the box that have a long /ū/ sound.

| | | | | |
|---|---|---|---|---|
| duke | dug | fuse | due | rule |
| vase | flute | like | duel | rude |
| fun | fume | meat | gum | fuel |
| tune | cute | boat | dune | lube |

**C** Write the correct word for each picture.

1. mule   mug

_____

2. late   lute

_____

3. tube   tub

_____

# ★ Phonics · Lesson 11

**D**  Circle eight words in the puzzle that have a long /ū/ sound. Then write the words on the lines.

| | | | | | | | | |
|---|---|---|---|---|---|---|---|---|
| W | B | F | U | E | L | P | Y | G |
| S | I | U | N | V | A | E | U | L |
| U | P | M | G | R | O | K | L | T |
| E | Z | E | D | U | N | E | E | B |
| C | J | M | U | C | L | P | H | X |
| F | S | Q | D | I | M | U | S | E |
| L | U | B | E | F | S | K | R | O |
| A | H | M | Q | I | N | D | Y | J |

_____

_____

_____

_____

_____

_____

_____

_____

**E**  Circle the word that makes sense in the sentence.

| | | | |
|---|---|---|---|
| 1. Sue had on a _____ hat. | cut | cap | cute |
| 2. At Yule time they _____ a big log. | own | ate | use |
| 3. Was that dude _____ to him? | rude | make | need |
| 4. In June we rode on a _____ . | meal | mule | mole |
| 5. Moe can play the _____ . | lube | lean | lute |
| 6. The fumes from the _____ were bad. | foe | fuel | sun |
| 7. When the lights went out, we looked at the _____ . | fuse | time | code |
| 8. The sky was a deep blue _____ . | hum | hue | hut |

# ★ Phonics · Lesson 11

★◆★◆★◆★◆★◆★◆★◆★◆★◆★◆★◆★◆★◆★◆★◆★◆★◆

**F** Write a synonym from the box for each word below. (A *synonym* is a word that has a similar meaning.)

| | | | | |
|---|---|---|---|---|
| cube | govern | fight | gas | funny |
| bare | pretty | color | hint | impolite |

**1.** fume _____

**2.** cue _____

**3.** rude _____

**4.** hue _____

**5.** duel _____

**6.** cute _____

**7.** rule _____

**8.** nude _____

**G** Write an answer to each riddle. Use the words in the box.

| | | | | | |
|---|---|---|---|---|---|
| lute | rave | cube | fuel | rule | duke |
| jug | mule | June | tube | tune | dune |

**1.** I am burned for heat. What am I? _____

**2.** I am something you sing. What am I? _____

**3.** I am an animal you can ride. What am I? _____

**4.** I am a geometric shape. What am I? _____

**5.** I am something that tells you what to do. What am I? _____

**6.** I am a summer month. What am I? _____

**7.** I am something you play music on. What am I? _____

**8.** I am by a sandy beach. What am I? _____

**9.** I am inside a paper roll. What am I? _____

**10.** I am a nobleman. What am I? _____

# ★ Phonics · Lesson 12

## R-Controlled Vowels

The letter *r* changes the sound of a vowel.

jar     bird     fern     corn

nurse     hair     pear     mare

**A** Write *ar, ir, or, er,* or *ur* to complete the words in each sentence. Use the words from the box.

| | | | | | |
|---|---|---|---|---|---|
| purse | horn | curb | herd | surf | worked |
| dart | tar | park | hard | car | jerk |
| form | curl | force | dirt | bird | farm |

1. Burt will p ___ ___ k the c ___ ___ at the c ___ ___ b.

2. Kirk w ___ ___ ked h ___ ___ d on the f ___ ___ m.

3. The f ___ ___ m of the h ___ ___ n was a c ___ ___ l.

4. Gert got d ___ ___ t and t ___ r on her p ___ ___ se.

5. The f ___ ___ ce of the s ___ ___ f hit the b ___ ___ d.

**B** Write the past tense of each verb below.

1. wear _____     2. bear _____     3. tear _____

**C** Write the correct word for each picture.

1.     bar     barn

2.     cork     core

3.     dirt     dart

_____     _____     _____

# ★ Phonics · Lesson 12

**D** **Write a synonym from the box for each word below. (A *synonym* is a word that has a similar meaning.)**

| woof | gal | jerk | wool | rude | wagon |
|------|-----|------|------|------|-------|
| attract | curse | carnival | shape | rope | piece |

**1.** cord _____

**2.** lure _____

**3.** fair _____

**4.** curt _____

**5.** form _____

**6.** part _____

**7.** bark _____

**8.** yarn _____

**9.** cart _____

**10.** girl _____

**E** **Circle the correct homophone for each word meaning. (A *homophone* sounds like another word but has a different meaning and a different spelling.)**

| | | |
|---|---|---|
| **1.** a large furry animal | bare | bear |
| **2.** an evergreen tree | fir | fur |
| **3.** money that you pay for a ride | fair | fare |
| **4.** a kind of fruit | pear | pare |
| **5.** grows on top of your head | hare | hair |
| **6.** what you do with clothes | wear | ware |
| **7.** something that is mined | or | ore |
| **8.** before | fore | for |

# ★ Phonics · Lesson 12

 **Use the clues to complete the puzzle. Hint: each answer is a word with an _r_-controlled vowel sound.**

### ACROSS

**3.** a pocketbook

**4.** to hurt someone

**6.** a word for _either_

**7.** opposite of _boy_

**8.** unusual

**9.** opposite of _less_

**10.** big group of cows

### DOWN

**1.** comes from your eyes when you cry

**2.** like a rabbit

**3.** take the skin off fruit

**4.** large animal with a mane

**5.** a scratch or stain

**7.** it can make you sick

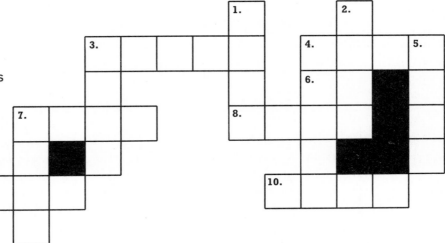

 **Write an answer to each riddle. Use the words from the box.**

| verb | furl | card | park | fort |
|------|------|------|------|------|
| air | forty | tar | perk | harp |

**1.** I am a musical instrument with strings. What am I? _____

**2.** I am a safe place for soldiers. What am I? _____

**3.** I am what you breathe. What am I? _____

**4.** I am a part of speech. What am I? _____

**5.** I am a number after 39. What am I? _____

**6.** I am a place to play. What am I? _____

**7.** I am black and sticky. What am I? _____

# ★ Phonics · Lesson 13

## Vowel Sounds OI/OY and OU/OW

The letters *oi* and *oy* can spell the same vowel sound.

coin          boy

The letters *ow* and *ou* can spell the same vowel sound.

cow          house

**A**  Read the words in the box. Write each word in the correct place on the chart.

| count | coy | down | foil | fowl | join | jowl | loin |
| oink | round | sour | soy | tout | toy | wow | |

**oi/oy**  _____  _____  _____

_____  _____  _____

**ou/ow**  _____  _____  _____

_____  _____  _____

**B**  Change the vowel pairs in each word to make a word that has the vowel sound in *joy* or *cow*.

**1.** load ➜ l ___ ___ d

**2.** seal ➜ s ___ ___ l

**3.** tail ➜ t ___ ___ l

**4.** boat ➜ b ___ ___ t

**5.** gain ➜ g ___ ___ n

**6.** ear ➜ ___ ___ r

**C**  Write the correct word for each picture.

**1.**          mouse     mice          _____

**2.**          germ     gown          _____

**3.**          eel     oil          _____

# ★ Phonics · Lesson 13

**D**  Draw a line to match each word on the left to a synonym on the right. (A *synonym* is a word that has a similar meaning)

1. howl

2. coil

3. joy

4. gown

5. join

6. rout

7. boy

8. toil

9. vow

10. soil

a. **defeat**

b. **dirt**

c. **dress**

d. **guy**

e. **yell**

f. **promise**

g. **link**

h. **wind**

i. **happiness**

j. **work**

**PHONICS ALERT!**

The letters *ow* have two sounds:

1: /ow/ in **down**

2: long /o/ in **low**

**E**  Write *yes* or *no* to answer each question.

1. Can a coin point? _____

2. Can a sow oink? _____

3. Can a toy have a voice? _____

4. Can fowl make a noise? _____

5. Can a boy be loud? _____

6. Can a gown pout? _____

**F**  Write a sentence of your own using each of these words.

1. how _____

2. boil _____

3. out _____

# ★ Phonics · Lesson 13

**G** Write an antonym from the box for each word below. (An *antonym* is a word that has the opposite meaning.)

| boil | bow | boy | down | joy |
|------|-----|-----|------|-----|
| loud | now | sour | toil | town |

**1.** relax _____

**2.** sweet _____

**3.** sadness _____

**4.** soft _____

**5.** then _____

**6.** up _____

**7.** country _____

**8.** girl _____

**H** Write an answer to each riddle. Use the words in the box.

| bow | foul | hour | howl | joint | mouse |
|-----|------|------|------|-------|-------|
| oil | owl | soil | soy | town | toy |

**1.** I am 60 minutes. What am I? _____

**2.** I am called in basketball games. What am I? _____

**3.** I am a fuel. What am I? _____

**4.** I am a sauce for Chinese food. What am I? _____

**5.** I am a large bird. What am I? _____

**6.** I am a community. What am I? _____

**7.** I am where two bones meet. What am I? _____

**8.** I am the front of a boat. What am I? _____

**9.** I am something you play with. What am I? _____

**10.** I am a small gray animal. What am I? _____

# ★ Phonics · Lesson 14

### Vowel Sounds of OO

The letters *oo* can spell the vowel sound in *moose*.     moose

The letters *oo* can spell the vowel sound in *book*.     book

**A** **Read each pair of words. Write the words with the /o͞o/ sound in room.**

**PHONICS ALERT!**

**ew**

The letters *oo* also spell the /o͞o/ sound found in **new**.

1. book   boom   _____

2. hood   hoot   _____

3. foot   fool   _____

4. tool   took   _____

5. goof   good   _____

6. loop   look   _____

**B** **Write the correct word for each picture.**

1.   hoop   hook

_____

2.   moon   moose

_____

3.   roof   rook

_____

**C** **Read the words in the box. Write the words in the correct place on the chart.**

| good | wood | noon | ooze | foot | cook |
| fool | soon | nook | look | zoom | loose |

| /o͞o/ in loom | _____ | _____ | _____ |
| | _____ | _____ | _____ |
| /oo/ in took | _____ | _____ | _____ |
| | _____ | _____ | _____ |

# ★ Phonics · Lesson 14

**D** Write a word from the box to rhyme with each underlined word.

| book | down | school | goose | Zoom |
|------|------|--------|-------|------|
| hood | zoo | coil | mood | noon |

1. A _____ rule

2. _____ around the room

3. In the _____ for food

4. It will soon be _____ .

5. A new _____

6. He took the _____ .

7. A good _____

8. A loose _____

**E** Each of the words below stands for a sound. Write who or what might make each sound.

1. coo _____

2. boom _____

3. toot _____

4. moo _____

5. boo _____

6. hoot _____

## PHONICS ALERT!

**ou**

The letters *ou* spell the /o͞o/ sound in **soup** and the /ou/ sound in **loud**.

**F** Write *yes* or *no* to answer each question.

1. Is a roof made of wool? _____

2. Can a fool goof? _____

3. Can a cook read a book? _____

4. Is a pool cool? _____

5. Is a boot for a foot? _____

6. Can goo ooze? _____

# ★ Phonics · Lesson 14

◆ ★ ◆ ★ ◆ ★ ◆ ★ ◆ ★ ◆ ★ ◆ ★ ◆ ★ ◆ ★ ◆ ★ ◆ ★ ◆ ★ ◆ ★ ◆ ★ ◆ ★ ◆

**G** **Write a synonym from the box for each word below. (A *synonym* is a word that has a similar meaning.)**

| chilly | to | chef | peek | fine |
|--------|-----|------|------|------|
| lumber | midday | also | soot | seep |

**1.** too _____

**2.** cool _____

**3.** look _____

**4.** good _____

**5.** ooze _____

**6.** noon _____

**7.** cook _____

**8.** wood _____

**H** **Write an answer for each riddle. Use the words from the box.**

| soot | foot | root | loom | moose | toot |
|------|------|------|------|-------|------|
| book | pool | moon | boot | zoo | goose |

**1.** I am something you read. What am I? _____

**2.** I am part of a plant. What am I? _____

**3.** I am something you swim in. What am I? _____

**4.** I am a park with animals. What am I? _____

**5.** I am a kind of fowl. What am I? _____

**6.** I am something you wear on your foot. What am I? _____

**7.** I am something you use to weave. What am I? _____

**8.** I am in the night sky. What am I? _____

**9.** I am found in fireplaces. What am I? _____

**10.** I am a large animal with antlers. What am I? _____

# ★ Phonics · Lesson 15

## Other Vowel Sounds

The letters *al, all, aw,* and *au* can spell the vowel sound /ô/ in *ball.*

salt          ball          auto          hawk

**A**  Read each pair of words. Write the word with the vowel sound /ô/ in ball.

1. jaunt   joint   _____    4. tall   tale   _____

2. hail   haul   _____    5. heat   halt   _____

3. pow   paw   _____    6. cue   caw   _____

**B**  Read the words in the box. Write the words in the correct place on the chart.

| call | autumn | talk | haunt | gawk | yawn |
|------|--------|------|-------|------|------|
| cause | bawl | all | fault | hall | lawn |

| aw | _____  _____  _____  _____ |
|------|------|
| au | _____  _____  _____  _____ |
| al/all | _____  _____  _____  _____ |

**C**  Write the correct word for each picture.

1. farm   fawn          2. wail   wall          3. voice   vault

_____    _____    _____

# ★ Phonics · Lesson 15

**D** **Circle the word that makes sense in the sentence.**

| | | | |
|---|---|---|---|
| **1.** Dad ____ Paul to play ball. | taunt | taught | tight |
| **2.** Do not walk on the ____ . | lawn | law | late |
| **3.** Did Saul ____ at the play? | yard | yes | yawn |
| **4.** Let's walk to the ____ . | male | mall | made |
| **5.** How ____ is the wall? | tail | team | tall |
| **6.** She has ____ on her jaw. | saw | sauce | some |

**E** **Write the past tense for these words.**

**1.** catch _____        **2.** teach _____

**F** **Circle the correct homophone for each word meaning. (A *homophone* sounds like another word but has a different meaning and a different spelling.)**

| | | |
|---|---|---|
| **1.** a dog's feet | pause | paws |
| **2.** to carry something | hall | haul |
| **3.** the reason something happens | caws | cause |
| **4.** a place with many stores | mall | maul |
| **5.** to cry hard | ball | bawl |
| **6.** a kind of tool | awl | all |

# ★ Phonics · Lesson 15

**G** **Write an antonym from the box for each word below. (An *antonym* is a word that has the opposite meaning.)**

| | | | | |
|---|---|---|---|---|
| bawl | call | salt | dawn | gawk |
| gaunt | halt | raw | tall | fall |

1. short    _____

2. chubby    _____

3. proceed    _____

4. pepper    _____

5. sunset    _____

6. laugh    _____

7. cooked    _____

8. spring    _____

**H** **Write an answer to each riddle. Use the words in the box.**

| | | | | | |
|---|---|---|---|---|---|
| pawn | pause | gauze | wall | ball | law |
| fault | sauce | lawn | jaw | fawn | hawk |

1. I divide things. What am I? _____

2. I am used in bandages. What am I? _____

3. I am where grass grows. What am I? _____

4. I am a large bird. What am I? _____

5. I am a baby deer. What am I? _____

6. I make food taste good. What am I? _____

7. I am part of your face. What am I? _____

8. I am something you obey. What am I? _____

9. I am a chess piece. What am I? _____

10. I am used in many sports. What am I? _____

# ★ Phonics · Lesson 16

## Blends With R

In a consonant blend, you hear the sound of each consonant. Consonant blends with the letter *r* include *br, cr, dr, fr, gr, pr,* and *tr*.

broom          crown          drum          frog

**A** **Read each pair of words. Write the word that begins with a consonant blend.**

1. tap   trap        _____
2. bread   bead      _____
3. prop   pop        _____
4. gay   gray        _____

5. gave   grave      _____
6. frame   fame      _____
7. drip   dip        _____
8. bake   brake      _____

**B** **Change the blend in each word below to make a new word.**

1. Change *gr* to *cr*

greed → _____

grew → _____

grab → _____

2. Change *br* to *fr*

breeze → _____

brown → _____

bright → _____

3. Change *tr* to *dr*

trip → _____

troop → _____

train → _____

**C** **Write the correct word for each picture.**

1.

room   groom

_____

2.

tray   trap

_____

3.

prize   pride

_____

# ★ Phonics · Lesson 16

**D** Write a synonym from the box for each word below. (A *synonym* is a word that has a similar meaning.)

| dull | trace | weak | jab | bawl | cut |
|------|-------|------|-----|------|-----|
| smile | creep | fight | gust | pull | path |

1. brawl _____

2. trim _____

3. crawl _____

4. drag _____

5. grin _____

6. breeze _____

7. prod _____

8. drab _____

9. frail _____

10. trail _____

**E** Write the present tense of each verb below.

1. grew _____

2. drove _____

3. drew _____

4. broke _____

**F** Write a tongue twister sentence using at least three words with each of these blends.

1. br _____

2. gr _____

3. tr _____

# ★ Phonics · Lesson 16

**G**  **Circle the correct blend to complete the word in each sentence. Then write the blend in the word.**

1. Bret will ____eet us at the train.           **tr**      **gr**      **dr**

2. Grace was ____ave when she broke her arm.     **br**      **cr**      **fr**

3. Did the frog ____oak?                         **fr**      **pr**      **cr**

4. Dad had a lot of ____aise for Brad.           **cr**      **pr**      **dr**

5. Fred got a ____eat for his pet crow.          **br**      **tr**      **dr**

6. Fran had a fright from a bad ____eam.         **dr**      **pr**      **cr**

**H**  **Write an answer to each riddle. Use the words from the box.**

| price | grape | bread | trout | drape | brook |
|-------|-------|-------|-------|-------|-------|
| brain | frame | crib  | crow  | green | crane |

1. I am a kind of fish. What am I? _____

2. I am a kind of fruit. What am I? _____

3. I am what you put a picture in. What am I? _____

4. I am the color of most plants. What am I? _____

5. I am at a window. What am I? _____

6. I am a tall building machine. What am I? _____

7. I am a kind of bird. What am I? _____

8. I am how much something costs. What am I? _____

9. I am a baby's bed. What am I? _____

10. I am a small stream. What am I? _____

# ★ Phonics · Lesson 17

## Blends With S

In a consonant blend, you hear the sound of each consonant. Consonant blends with the letter s include *sc, sk, sm, sn, sp, st,* and *sw.*

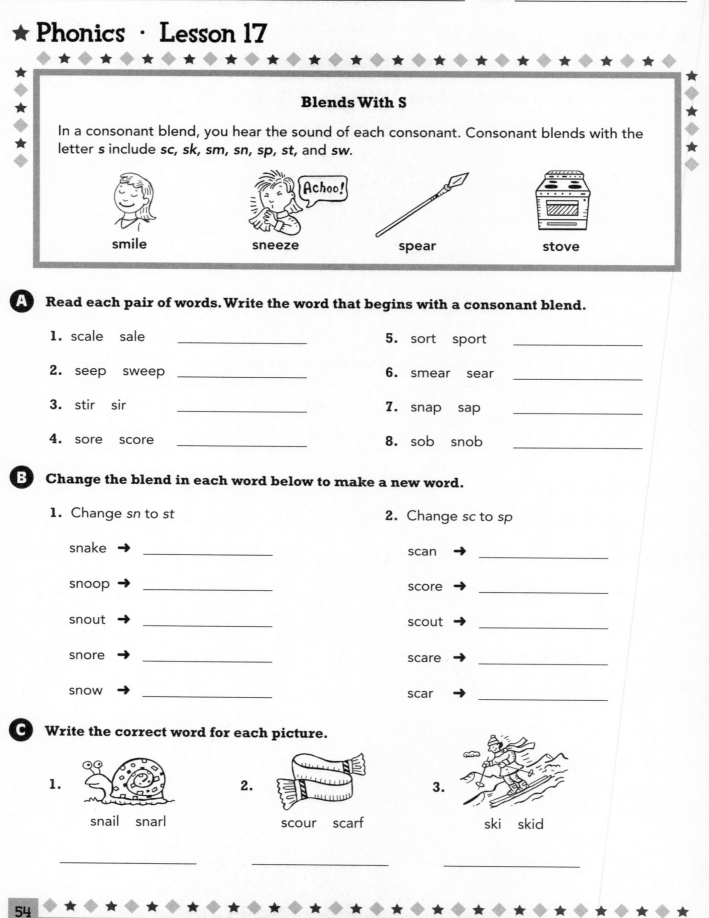

smile          sneeze          spear          stove

**A** Read each pair of words. Write the word that begins with a consonant blend.

1. scale   sale   _____

2. seep   sweep   _____

3. stir   sir   _____

4. sore   score   _____

5. sort   sport   _____

6. smear   sear   _____

7. snap   sap   _____

8. sob   snob   _____

**B** Change the blend in each word below to make a new word.

1. Change *sn* to *st*

snake ➜ _____

snoop ➜ _____

snout ➜ _____

snore ➜ _____

snow ➜ _____

2. Change *sc* to *sp*

scan ➜ _____

score ➜ _____

scout ➜ _____

scare ➜ _____

scar ➜ _____

**C** Write the correct word for each picture.

1. snail   snarl

2. scour   scarf

3. ski   skid

# ★ Phonics · Lesson 17

**D** **Write each group of words below in alphabetical order.**

1. space _____

   smart _____

   stone _____

   scab _____

   sneak _____

   sky _____

2. storm _____

   step _____

   stalk _____

   stain _____

   stub _____

   steam _____

**E** **Write the present tense of each word below.**

1. spoke _____    3. swam _____

2. sped _____     4. spun _____

**F** **Write a tongue twister using at least three words with each of these blends.**

1. sn _____

2. st _____

3. sp _____

# ★ Phonics · Lesson 17

**G**  Circle the correct blend to complete the word in each sentence. Then write the blend in the word.

1. Steve got a scoop of ____eet ice cream.          sn          sw          sc

2. Stella will sweep the ____ore.                    sk          sp          st

3. Will Stan star in the ____it?                     sc          sn          sk

4. The high speed made the car skid and ____in.      sp          sw          sm

5. Stu spoke to the scout with a ____ile.            st          sn          sm

6. Did Skip drop his ____arf on the stoop?           sc          sm          st

**H**  Write an answer to each riddle. Use the words from the box.

| sky | spoon | stage | snake | smoke | skirt |
|-----|-------|-------|-------|-------|-------|
| swan | star | skate | snow | skin | scale |

1. I weigh things. What am I? _____

2. I am a shoe with wheels. What am I? _____

3. I am used for eating. What am I? _____

4. I am a bird that likes water. What am I? _____

5. I am come from fire. What am I? _____

6. I am a reptile. What am I? _____

7. I cover your body. What am I? _____

8. I am something girls wear. What am I? _____

9. I am soft and white. What am I? _____

10. I am where a play takes place. What am I? _____

# ★ Phonics · Lesson 18

## Blends With L

In a consonant blend, you hear the sound of each consonant. Consonant blends with the letter *l* include *bl, cl, fl, gl, pl,* and *sl.*

blouse            clown            flute            plane

**A** Read each pair of words. Write the word that begins with a consonant blend.

1. bob    blob    _____

2. gloat    goat    _____

3. club    cub    _____

4. pay    play    _____

5. flame    fame    _____

6. sight    slight    _____

7. boom    bloom    _____

8. fleet    feet    _____

**B** Change the blend in each word below to make a new word.

1. Change *fl* to *bl*

flood  ➜  _____

flare  ➜  _____

flight  ➜  _____

2. Change *gl* to *cl*

glad  ➜  _____

glue  ➜  _____

glean  ➜  _____

3. Change *sl* to *pl*

slum  ➜  _____

slug  ➜  _____

slot  ➜  _____

**C** Write the correct word for each picture.

1.

flat    flag

_____

2.

plow    plot

_____

3.

gloom    globe

_____

# ★ Phonics · Lesson 18

**D** Circle the correct homophone for each word meaning. (A *homophone* sounds like another word but has a different meaning and a different spelling.)

1. an illness                          flu          flew

2. flat land                          plane        plain

3. the past tense of *blow*            blue         blew

4. a tiny insect                       flee         flea

**E** Write an antonym from the box for each word below. (An *antonym* is a word that has the opposite meaning.)

| wither | work | pleased | ceiling | cloudy | open |
|--------|------|---------|---------|--------|------|
| sink | slide | wake | fast | curved | sad |

1. close _____          6. play _____

2. slow _____          7. bloom _____

3. clear _____          8. float _____

4. glad _____          9. floor _____

5. sleep _____          10. flat _____

**F** Write a tongue twister using at least three words with each of these blends.

1. fl _____

2. sl _____

3. cl _____

# ★ Phonics · Lesson 18

**G** Circle the correct blend to complete the word in each sentence. Then write the blend in the word.

1. Flo wore a blue ____ouse.                              pl      bl      sl

2. Did this place ____ease Clem?                          bl      fl      pl

3. Glen gave his claim to the ____erk.                    cl      gl      fl

4. Clair plans to make a clay ____ate.                    bl      pl      gl

5. A cut from the blade made Dad's finger ____eed.        bl      pl      cl

6. Sleet and snow added gloom to the ____oudy day.        gl      cl      sl

**H** Write the answer to each riddle. Use the words from the box.

| plum | clam | slide | claw | blob | brown |
|------|------|-------|------|------|-------|
| blue | flour | blood | cloak | sled | glue |

1. I have no shape. What am I? _____

2. I have runners that slide down hills. What am I? _____

3. I hold things together. What am I? _____

4. I am part of a bird. What am I? _____

5. I am used in baking. What am I? _____

6. I am a purple fruit. What am I? _____

7. I am like a coat. What am I? _____

8. I am shellfish. What am I? _____

9. I am the color of the sea. What am I? _____

10. I flow inside your body. What am?_____

# ★ Phonics · Lesson 19

### Three-Letter Blends

Some consonant blends have three letters. Consonant blends with three letters include *scr, squ, str, spr, spl,* and *thr.*

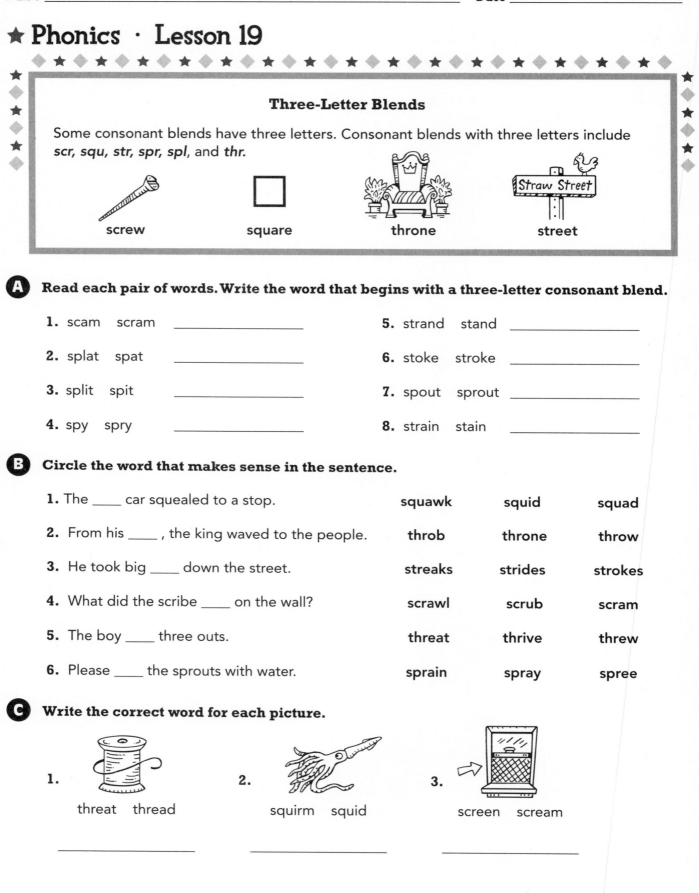

screw          square          throne          street

**A** **Read each pair of words. Write the word that begins with a three-letter consonant blend.**

**1.** scam   scram   _____

**2.** splat   spat   _____

**3.** split   spit   _____

**4.** spy   spry   _____

**5.** strand   stand   _____

**6.** stoke   stroke   _____

**7.** spout   sprout   _____

**8.** strain   stain   _____

**B** **Circle the word that makes sense in the sentence.**

**1.** The ____ car squealed to a stop.          **squawk**     **squid**     **squad**

**2.** From his ____ , the king waved to the people.     **throb**     **throne**     **throw**

**3.** He took big ____ down the street.          **streaks**     **strides**     **strokes**

**4.** What did the scribe ____ on the wall?      **scrawl**     **scrub**     **scram**

**5.** The boy ____ three outs.                  **threat**     **thrive**     **threw**

**6.** Please ____ the sprouts with water.        **sprain**     **spray**     **spree**

**C** **Write the correct word for each picture.**

**1.**          **2.**          **3.**

threat   thread          squirm   squid          screen   scream

_____          _____          _____

# ★ Phonics · Lesson 19

**D** Write a synonym from the box for each word below. (A *synonym* is a word that has a similar meaning.)

| split | scream | squab | squirm | spry | scrape |
|-------|--------|-------|--------|------|--------|
| sprig | throw | squirt | squad | street | stray |

**1.** rub _____

**2.** road _____

**3.** toss _____

**4.** spray _____

**5.** team _____

**6.** yell _____

**7.** divide _____

**8.** wiggle _____

**9.** nimble _____

**10.** wander _____

**E** Write each group of words below in alphabetical order.

**1.**
spread _____
scrap _____
splice _____
strip _____
threw _____
squeeze _____

**2.**
strum _____
stroke _____
strap _____
streak _____
stripe _____

**F** Write a tongue twister using at least three words with each of these blends.

**1.** thr _____

**2.** str _____

**3.** spr _____

# ★ Phonics · Lesson 19

**G** **Circle the correct blend to complete the word in each sentence. Then write the blend in the word.**

| | | | |
|---|---|---|---|
| **1.** She _____ead jam on a square of bread. | **thr** | **spr** | **scr** |
| **2.** The squid will _____irm on the dock. | **squ** | **thr** | **spl** |
| **3.** You strike a drum and _____um a guitar. | **spr** | **scr** | **str** |
| **4.** He _____ew the ball straight to me. | **spl** | **thr** | **squ** |
| **5.** A _____ay cat strode by. | **str** | **spr** | **thr** |
| **6.** The sprout will have to _____ain for sun. | **spl** | **str** | **spr** |

**H** **Write an answer to each riddle. Use the words from the box.**

| | | | | | |
|---|---|---|---|---|---|
| throne | scrap | three | stream | spruce | straw |
| screen | throat | splat | strike | thread | squeak |

**1.** I keep bugs from flying in windows. What am I? _____

**2.** I am a kind of evergreen tree. What am I? _____

**3.** I am used in sewing. What am I? _____

**4.** I am the sound a mouse makes. What am I? _____

**5.** I am a flowing body of water. What am I? _____

**6.** I am a leftover. What am I? _____

**7.** I am at the back of your mouth. What am I? _____

**8.** I am what a pitcher throws to hitters. What am I? _____

**9.** I am a seat for a queen. What am I? _____

**10.** I am found in a horse stable. What am I? _____

# ★ Phonics · Lesson 20

## Final Consonant Blends

Some words end in consonant blends. In a blend, you hear the sound of each consonant. Some final consonant blends include *ct*, *nt*, *ft*, *lt*, *nd*, *ld*, *lp*, *mp*, *nk sp*, *sk*, and *st*.

belt        ant        hound        ink

**A**  Read each pair of words. Write the word that ends with a consonant blend.

1. pat   pact        _____

2. boast   boat      _____

3. cold   cod        _____

4. lap   lamp        _____

5. fin   find        _____

6. raft   rat        _____

7. hint   hit        _____

8. gap   gasp        _____

### PHONICS ALERT!

The blends *sk*, *sp*, and *st* are found at the beginning and at the end of words:

Beginning:  **sk**ate   **sp**ot   **st**ar

End:  a**sk**   ga**sp**   be**st**

**B**  Write three words that rhyme with each word below.

1. link        2. rest        3. tint        4. gold        5. camp

_____  _____  _____  _____  _____

_____  _____  _____  _____  _____

_____  _____  _____  _____  _____

**C**  Write the correct word for each picture.

1.              2.              3.

net   nest        tent   ten        ball   bald

_____        _____        _____

# ★ Phonics · Lesson 20

◆ ★ ◆ ★ ◆ ★ ◆ ★ ◆ ★ ◆ ★ ◆ ★ ◆ ★ ◆ ★ ◆ ★ ◆ ★ ◆ ★ ◆ ★ ◆ ★ ◆ ★ ◆ ★ ◆ ★ ◆

**D**  **Write the past tense for each verb below.**

1. build _____

2. sink _____

3. bend _____

4. find _____

5. tell _____

6. lend _____

7. hold _____

8. sell _____

9. go _____

10. feel _____

**E**  **Write an antonym from the box for each word below. (An *antonym* is a word that has the opposite meaning.)**

| slow | pepper | gulp | opinion | worst | lose |
|------|--------|------|---------|-------|------|
| least | start | hard | hot | east | right |

1. fact _____

2. end _____

3. find _____

4. left _____

5. soft _____

6. cold _____

7. best _____

8. fast _____

9. salt _____

10. west _____

**F**  **Write *yes* or *no* to answer each question.**

1. Can paint be faint?  _____

2. Can a hound yelp?  _____

3. Can you dust a sound?  _____

4. Can a desk be old?  _____

5. Can you put junk in a dump?  _____

6. Can you mend ink?  _____

◆ ★ ◆ ★ ◆ ★ ◆ ★ ◆ ★ ◆ ★ ◆ ★ ◆ ★ ◆ ★ ◆ ★ ◆ ★ ◆ ★ ◆ ★ ◆ ★ ◆ ★ ◆ ★ ◆ ★ ◆ ★ ◆

# ★ Phonics · Lesson 20

**G** **Circle the correct blend to complete the word in each sentence. Then write the blend in the word.**

| | | | |
|---|---|---|---|
| 1. The mist came in fast at the coa_____ . | st | sp | sk |
| 2. The skater went up the ramp to ju_____ . | nk | st | mp |
| 3. Hank likes to dunk a hu_____ of cake. | nt | nd | nk |
| 4. The colt ran wild on the sa_____ . | ct | nd | lp |

**H** **Write an answer to each riddle. Use the words in the box.**

| hand | raft | tank | honk | kilt | mast |
|------|------|------|------|------|------|
| mask | rust | pound | dusk | cent | rent |

1. I am a tall post on a sailboat. What am I? _____

2. I am a time at the end of the day. What am I? _____

3. I am a part of your body. What am I? _____

4. I am what you pay to live somewhere. What am I? _____

5. I am something you wear on Halloween. What am I? _____

6. I am a noise a car horn makes. What am I? _____

7. I am a penny. What am I? _____

8. I am something that happens to metal. What am I? _____

9. I am something a Scottish man wears. What am I? _____

10. I am a platform that floats. What am I? _____

Name _____     Date _____

# ★ Phonics · Lesson 21

## Double Consonants

Some words have double consonants—two of the same consonant appear together. In words with double consonants, you hear only one consonant sound.

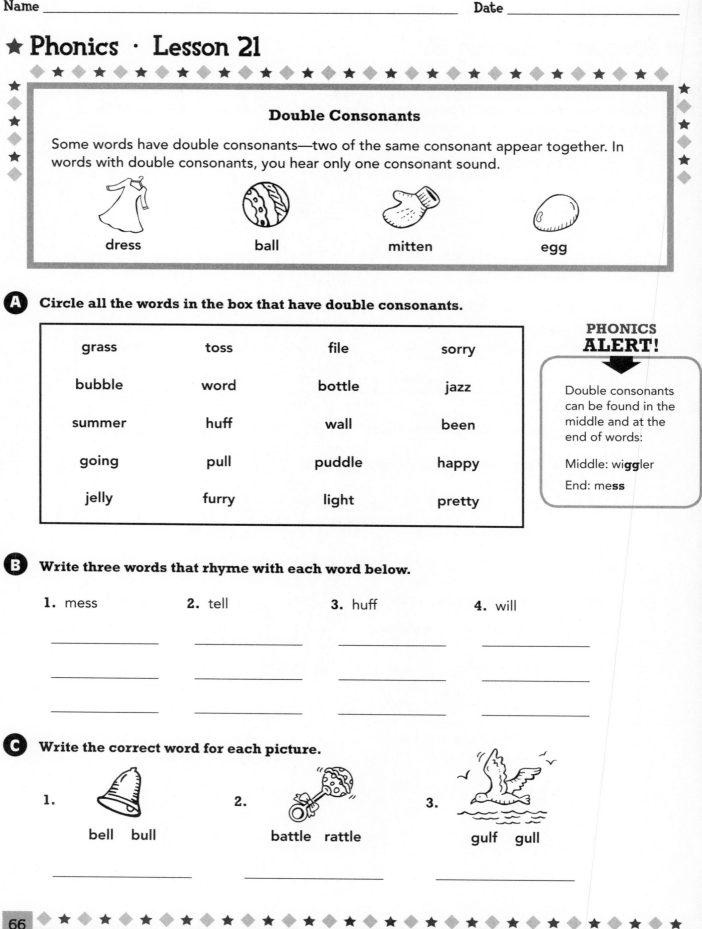

dress          ball          mitten          egg

**A** Circle all the words in the box that have double consonants.

| | | | |
|---|---|---|---|
| grass | toss | file | sorry |
| bubble | word | bottle | jazz |
| summer | huff | wall | been |
| going | pull | puddle | happy |
| jelly | furry | light | pretty |

**PHONICS ALERT!**

Double consonants can be found in the middle and at the end of words:

Middle: wi**gg**ler

End: me**ss**

**B** Write three words that rhyme with each word below.

1. mess          2. tell          3. huff          4. will

_____   _____   _____   _____

_____   _____   _____   _____

_____   _____   _____   _____

**C** Write the correct word for each picture.

1.               2.               3.

bell   bull          battle   rattle          gulf   gull

_____   _____   _____

# ★ Phonics · Lesson 21

**D** **Circle the correct homophone for each word meaning. (A *homophone* sounds like another word but has a different meaning and a different spelling.)**

| | | |
|---|---|---|
| 1. what a batter hits in baseball | **bawl** | **ball** |
| 2. a kind of fruit | **berry** | **bury** |
| 3. a phone | **sell** | **cell** |
| 4. something you might eat for breakfast | **roll** | **role** |
| 5. a corridor | **haul** | **hall** |

**E** **Each of the words below stands for a sound. Write who or what might make each sound.**

1. hiss _____

2. purr _____

3. buzz _____

4. fizz _____

**PHONICS ALERT!**

The consonants *j, k, q, w, x,* and *v* are not usually doubled.

**F** **Write a synonym from the box for each word below. (A *synonym* is a word that has a similar meaning.)**

| hurry | grass | buggy | cattle | pill | sniff |
|---|---|---|---|---|---|
| dinner | staff | pebble | scuff | little | battle |

| | |
|---|---|
| 1. stone _____ | 6. supper _____ |
| 2. carriage _____ | 7. tablet _____ |
| 3. lawn _____ | 8. smell _____ |
| 4. small _____ | 9. mark _____ |
| 5. fight _____ | 10. rush _____ |

# ★ Phonics · Lesson 21

**G** **Read the clues. Then fill in the LL puzzle.**

1. the season after summer

2. the opposite of short

3. a plant with red berries often seen in December

4. another way to say "hi"

5. the color of the sun

6. you put your head on it to sleep

1. ☐ ☐ L L
2. ☐ ☐ L L
3. ☐ ☐ L L ☐
4. ☐ ☐ L L ☐
5. ☐ ☐ L L ☐ ☐
6. ☐ ☐ L L ☐ ☐

**H** **Write an answer to each riddle. Use the words in the box.**

| lass | bull | doll | bill | sill | kitty |
|------|------|------|------|------|-------|
| puppy | apple | ladder | rabbit | cuff | kettle |

1. I am used for boiling water. What am I? _____

2. I am a furry animal with long ears. What am I? _____

3. I am a fruit that grows on a tree. What am I? _____

4. I am a young cat. What am I? _____

5. I am a girl. What am I? _____

6. I am something you climb. What am I? _____

7. I am at the end of a sleeve. What am I? _____

8. I am a toy that has clothes. What am I? _____

9. I am a large animal with horns. What am I? _____

10. I am under a window. What am I? _____

# ★ Phonics · Lesson 22

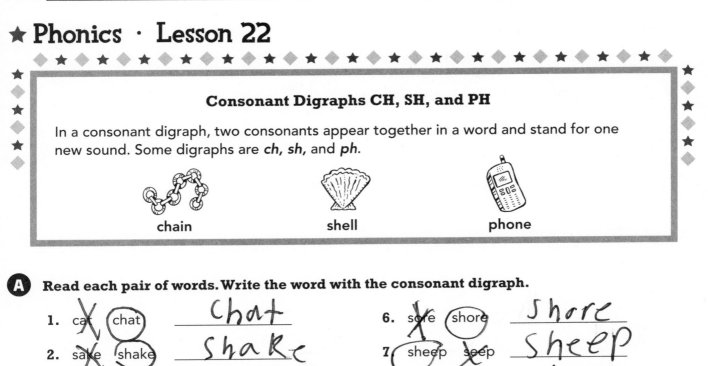

## Consonant Digraphs CH, SH, and PH

In a consonant digraph, two consonants appear together in a word and stand for one new sound. Some digraphs are *ch*, *sh*, and *ph*.

chain          shell          phone

**A** Read each pair of words. Write the word with the consonant digraph.

1. cat  (chat)     _Chat_
2. sake (shake)    _shake_
3. (shave) save    _shave_
4. pony (phony)    _Phony_
5. hip (chip)      _chip_

6. sore (shore)    _Shore_
7. (sheep) seep    _sheep_
8. (chase) (case)  _chase_
9. (chow) cow      _chow_
10. (ship) sip     _ship_

**B** Write three words that rhyme with each word below.

1. lunch
   _buch_
   _crouch_
   _much_

2. beach
   _eeach_
   _reach_
   _creach_
   _bleach_

3. dash
   _~~wish~~_
   _~~list~~_
   _cash_
   _bash_
   _mash_

 **C** Write the correct word for each picture

1. soup (shoe) ✓
   _shoe_

2. (photo) port
   _photo_

3. creep (cheese) ✓
   _cheese_

# ★ Phonics · Lesson 22

★ ◆ ★ ◆ ★ ◆ ★ ◆ ★ ◆ ★ ◆ ★ ◆ ★ ◆ ★ ◆ ★ ◆ ★ ◆ ★ ◆ ★ ◆ ★ ◆ ★ ◆ ★ ◆

**D** **Write an antonym from the box for each word below. (An *antonym* is a word that has the opposite meaning.)**

| chubby | rich | punch | fresh | push | chill |
|--------|------|-------|-------|------|-------|
| champ | sharp | she | shop | teach | shut |

1. learn _____

2. pull _____

3. dull _____

4. skinny _____

5. stale _____

6. open _____

7. poor _____

8. heat _____

9. he _____

10. loser _____

**E** **Circle the correct homophone for each word meaning. (A *homophone* sounds like another word but has a different meaning and a different spelling.)**

1. to crush food with your teeth          choo          chew

2. not costing too much          cheep          cheap

3. a kind of tree          beech          beach

4. something you wear on your foot          shoo          shoe

5. past tense of *shine*          shown          shone

**F** **Write a tongue twister using at least three words with each of these consonant digraphs.**

1. ch _____

_____

_____

2. sh _____

_____

_____

## PHONICS ALERT!

The consonant digraphs *ch*, *sh*, and *ph* can appear at the beginning, middle, and end of a word.

Beginning:  **ch**ess          **sh**ot          **ph**one

Middle:  lun**ch**room     fi**sh**net     gra**ph**ic

End:  mu**ch**          mu**sh**          gra**ph**

★ ◆ ★ ◆ ★ ◆ ★ ◆ ★ ◆ ★ ◆ ★ ◆ ★ ◆ ★ ◆ ★ ◆ ★ ◆ ★ ◆ ★ ◆ ★ ◆ ★ ◆

Name _____  Date _____

# ★ Phonics · Lesson 22

◆★◆★◆★◆★◆★◆★◆★◆★◆★◆★◆★◆★◆★◆★◆★◆

**G** Read the clues. Then fill in the puzzle. Each word has the digraph *ch* or *sh* in it.

1. how you might eat crackers.

2. food to put on crackers

3. a fuzzy fruit that grows on trees

4. a midday meal

5. food that comes from the sea

6. what a boxer does

7. a _____ of grapes

1. M □ □ □ □
2. □ □ E □ □ □
3. □ □ A □ □
4. L □ □ □ □
5. F □ □ □
6. □ U □ □
7. □ □ N □ □

**H** Write an answer to each riddle. Use the words in the box.

| chin | graph | pinch | phase | cheer | trash |
|------|-------|-------|-------|-------|-------|
| wish | inch | shin | sheet | shade | cash |

1. I am something you look for when it's hot. What am I? _____

2. I am a kind of chart. What am I? _____

3. I am on your bed. What am I? _____

4. I am what you throw away. What am I? _____

5. I am the lower part of your face. What am I? _____

6. I am what you make when you see a star. What am I? _____

7. I am what you do when your team wins. What am I? _____

8. I am dollars and cents. What am I? _____

9. I am a measurement on a ruler. What am I? _____

10. I am part of your leg. What am I? _____

# ★ Phonics · Lesson 23

## Consonant Digraphs TH, WH, NG, and GH

In a consonant digraph, two consonants appear together in a word and stand for one new sound. Some digraphs are *th*, *wh*, *ng*, and *gh*.

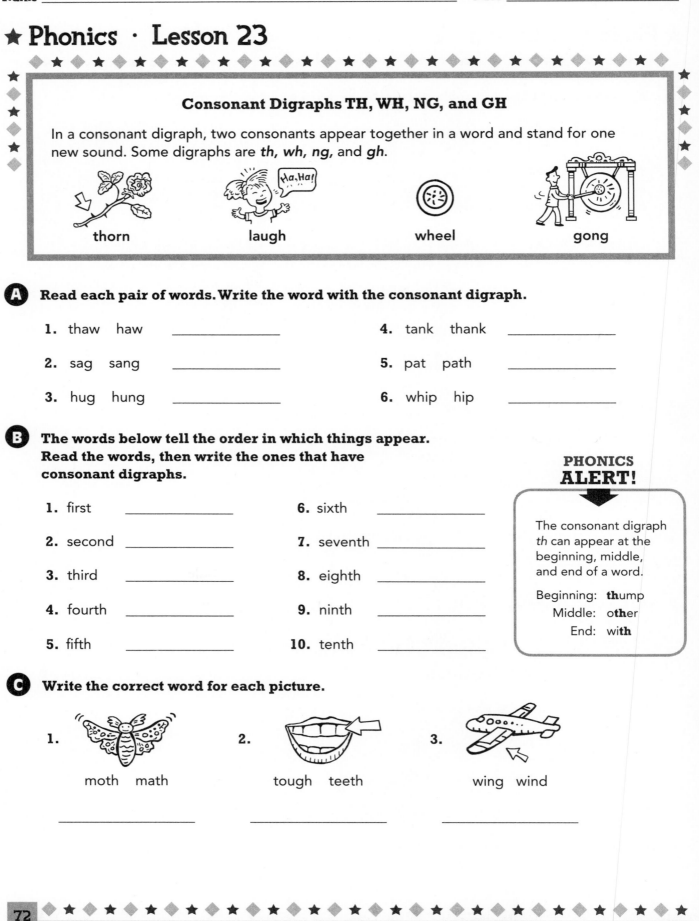

thorn          laugh          wheel          gong

**A** **Read each pair of words. Write the word with the consonant digraph.**

1. thaw   haw   _____

2. sag   sang   _____

3. hug   hung   _____

4. tank   thank   _____

5. pat   path   _____

6. whip   hip   _____

**B** **The words below tell the order in which things appear. Read the words, then write the ones that have consonant digraphs.**

1. first   _____

2. second   _____

3. third   _____

4. fourth   _____

5. fifth   _____

6. sixth   _____

7. seventh   _____

8. eighth   _____

9. ninth   _____

10. tenth   _____

### PHONICS ALERT!

The consonant digraph *th* can appear at the beginning, middle, and end of a word.

Beginning: **th**ump
Middle: o**th**er
End: wi**th**

**C** **Write the correct word for each picture.**

1. moth   math

_____

2. tough   teeth

_____

3. wing   wind

_____

# ★ Phonics · Lesson 23

**D** **Write the past tense for each verb below.**

1. hang _____

2. fling _____

3. sing _____

4. swing _____

5. bring _____

6. cling _____

**E** **Circle the correct homophone for each word meaning. (A *homophone* sounds like another word but has a different meaning and a different spelling.)**

| | | |
|---|---|---|
| 1. not smooth | ruff | rough |
| 2. wears a pointed black hat | witch | which |
| 3. belonging to them | there | their |
| 4. a large sea mammal | whale | wail |
| 5. to have on your body | where | wear |
| 6. something that's forecast daily | whether | weather |
| 7. jewelry for the finger | wring | ring |
| 8. cry or complain | whine | wine |
| 9. complete | hole | whole |
| 10. an amount of time | while | wile |

**F** **Write the consonant digraph in each of the words below.**

1. daughter _____

2. hunger _____

3. within _____

4. laughter _____

5. jungle _____

6. gather _____

# ★ Phonics · Lesson 23

◆★◆★◆★◆★◆★◆★◆★◆★◆★◆★◆★◆★◆★◆★◆

**G**  **Read the clues. Then fill in the TH puzzle.**

1. another word for mom

2. someone who writes books

3. another word for dad

4. the opposite of sister

5. a robber

1. ☐ ☐ T H ☐ ☐

2. ☐ ☐ T H ☐ ☐

3. ☐ ☐ T H ☐ ☐

4. ☐ ☐ ☐ T H ☐ ☐

5. T H ☐ ☐ ☐

**H**  **Write an answer to each riddle. Use the words in the box.**

| thirty | song | spring | young | wheat | tough |
|--------|------|--------|-------|-------|-------|
| hangar | king | prong | north | laugh | math |

1. I am part of a fork. What am I? _____

2. I am what you do when something is funny. What am I? _____

3. I am a number after 29. What am I? _____

4. I am something you sing. What am I? _____

5. I am a grain used in making bread. What am I? _____

6. I am the season before summer. What am I? _____

7. I am a ruler of a country. What am I? _____

8. I am a subject you have in school. What am I? _____

9. I am a direction. What am I? _____

10. I am a place for planes. What am I? _____

◆★◆★◆★◆★◆★◆★◆★◆★◆★◆★◆★◆★◆★◆★◆

# ★ Phonics · Lesson 24

## Silent Consonants

Many words have silent consonants. These letters are not pronounced.

**knob** (silent k)          **thumb** (silent b)          **rhino** (silent h)

**A**  **Read each pair of words. Write the word that has a silent consonant.**

1. keel   kneel   _____

2. wriggle   wiggle   _____

3. numb   nub   _____

4. ghost   host   _____

5. knew   new   _____

6. cold   could   _____

**B**  **Say each word. Write the silent consonant in the word.**

1. rhumba   _____

2. palm   _____

3. calm   _____

4. walk   _____

5. corps   _____

6. gnat   _____

7. known   _____

8. bomb   _____

9. oh   _____

10. honor   _____

**C**  **Write the correct word for each picture.**

1.          lamb   lab          _____

2.          kit   knit          _____

3.          writer   wreath          _____

# ★ Phonics · Lesson 24

**D** Write the past tense for each verb below.

1. write _____
2. wring _____
3. know _____

**E** Circle the correct homophone for each word meaning. (A *homophone* sounds like another word but has a different meaning and a different spelling.)

| | | |
|---|---|---|
| 1. the opposite of day | knight | night |
| 2. what a baker does to dough | need | knead |
| 3. cover something up | wrap | rap |
| 4. a juicy purple fruit | plum | plumb |
| 5. sixty minutes | hour | our |
| 6. a building material from trees | would | wood |
| 7. result when rope ends are tied together | knot | not |
| 8. the opposite of yes | know | no |
| 9. an African antelope | knew | gnu |

**F** Write a synonym from the box for each word below. (A *synonym* is a word that has a similar meaning.)

| anger | branch | rap | bite |
|---|---|---|---|
| guilt | grind | wrong | still |

1. gnash _____
2. limb _____
3. calm _____

4. wrath _____
5. knock _____
6. gnaw _____

# ★ Phonics · Lesson 24

**G** **Read the clues. Then fill in the puzzle. Each word has a silent consonant in it.**

1. part of body between the hand and the arm
2. how you get up a mountain
3. what you do on your knees
4. a ship that has been sunk for a long time
5. how your toes feel when it's very cold
6. what you do on a cell phone

1. ☐ ☐ ☐ S ☐
2. ☐ ☐ I ☐ ☐
3. ☐ ☐ ☐ ☐ L
4. ☐ ☐ E ☐ ☐
5. N ☐ ☐ ☐
6. T ☐ ☐ ☐

**H** **Write an answer to each riddle. Use the words in the box.**

| knee | wrench | rhyme | wren | comb | crumb |
|------|--------|-------|------|------|-------|
| gnat | knife | calf | gnome | sign | half |

1. I am a tool for turning nuts and bolts. What am I? _____

2. I am leftover from a cookie. What am I? _____

3. I help keep your hair neat. What am I? _____

4. I am a baby cow. What am I? _____

5. I am where your leg bends. What am I? _____

6. I am a small bird. What am I? _____

7. I am one of two equal parts. What am I? _____

8. I am a tool that cuts things. What am I? _____

9. I am a flying insect. What am I? _____

10. I am along the road and give
    information to drivers. What am I? _____

# Answers

## LESSON 1

**Page 6: A.** 1. top 2. ten 3. bib 4. bed 5. pin 6. pup 7. leg 8. ax 9. tub 10. map **B. add a:** tap, tan, bad, pan, lag, tab; **add e:** pen, pep; **add i:** tip, tin, bid, pip; **add o:** bob, pop, log, ox, mop; **add u:** bub, bud, pun, lug **Page 7: C. short /a/:** ban, dam, gas, nag; **short /e/:** beg, den, let, gem **D. short /i/:** pig, sis, lip; **short /o/:** got, not, bog; **short/u/:** gum, mud, tug **E.** 1. bag 2. men 3. pig 4. lad 5. net 6. bin 7. us 8. man 9. Pop 10. lot **Page 8: F.** 1. top 2. father 3. unhappy 4. large 5. dark 6. insect 7. mother 8. sack 9. talk **G.** 1. bat 2. pen 3. bun 4. pug 5. tug 6. sun 7. ten 8. mug

## LESSON 2

**Page 9: A.** 1. van 2. cup 3. fox 4. hat 5. jet 6. keg 7. rat 8. hut 9. fin 10. rod **B. short /a/:** fat, had, rap, ram; **short/e/:** fed, yes, wet, hem; **short/i/:** rid, kit, zip, yip; **short/o/:** cog, jot, cod, hot; **short /u/:** rut, jug, hug, fun **Page 10: C.** 1. cat 2. ran 3. fox 4. fun 5. hot 6. hog 7. vet 8. wig 9. rug 10. yam **D.** 1. fix 2. cap 3. jog 4. ram 5. jam 6. hem 7. lap 8. hat 9. cup 10. fun **Page 11: E.** 1. run 2. barrel 3. tear 4. hat 5. chubby 6. smack 7. vigor 8. pitcher 9. wave **F.** 1. cod 2. fig 3. cud 4. vet 5. hen 6. wax 7. jet 8. fog

## LESSON 3

**Page 12: A.** 1. tape 2. pane 3. mate 4. vane 5. made 6. gape 7. rage 8. fade 9. fate 10. dame **B.** 2. face 3. rake 4. mane 6. cave 7. take 8. lane **C.** 1. rake 2. gate 3. maze **Page 13: D.** 1. late 2. game 3. race 4. haze 5. cake 6. wave 7. male 8. pane **E. Possible:** 1. mane, cane, lane 2. maze, haze, gaze 3. rage, page, sage **F.** 1. lace 2. wade 3. fake 4. rage 5. gape, 6. gave 7. ate 8. maze **Page 14: G.** 1. early 2. real 3. female 4. give 5. different 6. lose 7. wild 8. love **H.** 1. game 2. wave 3. vase 4. cake 5. mane 6. rake 7. vane 8. pane

## LESSON 4

**Page 15: A.** 1. paid 2. bait 3. gay 4. aid 5. may 6. hail 7. ray 8. fail 9. say 10. bay **B.** 1. wait 2. ray 4. wail 8. raid 9. bay **C.** 1. sail 2. vane 3. tail **Page 16: D.** 1. maid 2. hail 3. pane 4. wait 5. bay 6. game **E.** 1. speak 2. help 3. pause 4. hurt 5. cry 6. prison **F.** 1. fail 2. lay 3. sail 4. aid 5. mail 6. rain 7. pain 8. paid **Page 17: G.** 1. way 2. vain 3. mail 4. day 5. gain 6. jail 7. gay 8. bail **H.** 1. rain 2. tail 3. May 4. bait 5. pail 6. mail 7. maid 8. jay

## LESSON 5

**Page 18: A.** 1. dine 2. hide 3. kite 4. pine 5. dime 6. ride 7. site 8. fine 9. ripe 10. bite **B.** 1. lice 2. pike 5. mime 6. rite 7. like 8. vile **C.** 1. hive 2. bike 3. pipe **Page 19: D. long /ī/:** vice, rite, wipe, fife, tide, pike; **long /ā/:** tame, aim, raid, lay, gape, mate **E.** 1. nine 2. nice 3. life 4. bike 5. rise 6. pipe 7. site 8. tide 9. tile 10. five **F. Possible:** 1. mine, dine, fine 2. wide, side, tide 3. like, pike, hike **Page 20: G.** 1. mean 2. dislike 3. unripe 4. husband 5. unwise 6. narrow 7. fall 8. virtue 9. dead 10. yours **H.** 1. dice 2. fife 3. bike 4. kite 5. five 6. lime 7. dime 8. pine

## LESSON 6

**Page 21: A.** 1. bye 2. tight 3. dry 4. high 5. by 6. fry 7. right 8. sigh 9. rye 10. light **B.** pile, night, rice, dry, why, bite, light, bye, my, high, time, spy, fry, wise **C.** 1. cry 2. sight 3. tights **Page 22: D.** 1. my 2. by 3. sky 4. cry 5. fly 6. try 7. dry 8. Why **E.** 1. bye 2. light 3. night 4. tight 5. sky 6. dry 7. shy 8. high **F. Sentences will vary. Page 23: G.** spy, sly, why, dye, by, sigh **H.** 1. dye 2. sky 3. sight 4. rye 5. night 6. right 7. spy 8. fight

## LESSON 7

**Page 24: A.** 1. reed 2. wee 3. teen 4. bee 5. weed 6. me 7. peep 8. beep **B.** meek, peel, she, fee, keep, reel, deed, seep, week, feel, meet, beep, teen, peek **C.** 1. heel 2. jeep 3. seed **Page 25: D.** 1. veep 2. jeep 3. beep 4. deep 5. keep 6. peep 7. seep 8. weep **E.** 1. seen 2. fee 3. keep 4. need 5. feet 6. meet 7. be 8. see **Page 26: F. heed:** need, feed, weed, deed, seed, reed; **week:** leek, meek, peek, reek **G.** 1. peep 2. eel 3. weed 4. bee 5. week 6. tee 7. teen 8. beet

## LESSON 8

**Page 27: A.** 1. read 2. lead 3. seat 4. neat 5. beat 6. meat 7. peat 8. bead **B.** 1. deal 2. neat 4. keep 6. we 7. kitty 9. heap 10. sea 11. be 12. funny **C.** 1. bean 2. tea 3. leap **Page 28: D.** leek, seek, meek, reek, peek, leak, week, peak **E.** 1. meat 2. weak 3. heel 4. team 5. real 6. peal 7. tea 8. peak 9. leak 10. sea **Page 29: F.** 1. jay 2. bunny 3. kitty 4. mice 5. seal 6. eel 7. geese **G.** 1. meal 2. leaf 3. heap 4. baby 5. taffy 6. pea 7. city 8. seat 9. heat 10. seam

## LESSON 9

**Page 30: A.** 1. code 2. note 3. mope 4. rode 5. lobe 6. hope 7. pope 8. rote **B.** 1. cope 2. pole 3. pope 4. rote 5. mole 6. cove 7. woke 8. lone 9. rope 10. dome **C.** 1. robe 2. nose 3. bone **Page 31: D.** 1. cope 2. dome 3. cove 4. vote 5. hole 6. rose 7. code 8. poke **E. Possible:** 1. zone, lone, cone, bone 2. hole, mole, sole, pole 3. mope, lope, cope, pope **F.** 1. weave 2. ride 3. wake 4. dive **Page 32: G.** 1. sulk 2. jab 3. elect 4. want 5. opening 6. area 7. single 8. part **H.** 1. rope 2. note 3. home 4. hose 5. sole 6. dome 7. cone 8. lobe

## LESSON 10

**Page 33: A.** go, tow, doe, roam, load, boat, yoke, moan, coal, dole, owe, goat, hoe, foam **B.** 1. loan 2. boat 3. foal 4. moan 5. road 6. moat 7. goat 8. soap 9. soak 10. bowl **C.** 1. foal 2. row 3. goat **Pages 34: D.** 1. soak 2. so 3. low 4. roam 5. own 6. mow 7. foe 8. go **E.** 1. road 2. tow 3. loan 4. load 5. hoe **F.** Sentences will vary. **Page 35: G.** so, oat, row, foe, low, mow, no, woe, toe **H.** 1. coal 2. bow 3. bowl 4. soap 5. goal 6. moat 7. coat 8. oak 9. loaf 10. moan

## LESSON 11

**Page 36: A.** 1. dude 2. use 3. jute 4. fuse 5. cube 6. cute **B.** duke, fuse, due, rule, flute, rude, duel, fume, fuel, tune, cute, dune, lube **C.** 1. mule 2. lute, 3. tube **Page 37: D.** fuel, dune, muse, lube, sue, fume, Yule, dude **E.** 1. cute 2. use 3. rude 4. mule 5. lute 6. fuel 7. fuse. 8. hue **Page 38: F.** 1. gas 2. hint 3. impolite 4. color 5. fight 6. pretty 7. govern 8. bare **G.** 1. fuel 2. tune 3. mule 4. cube 5. rule 6. June 7. lute 8. dune 9. tube 10. duke

## LESSON 12

**Page 39: A.** 1. park, car, curb 2. worked, hard, farm 3. form, horn, curl, 4. dirt, tar, purse 5. force, surf, bird **B.** 1. wore 2. bore 3. tore **C.** 1. barn 2. cork 3. dart **Page 40: D.** 1. rope 2. attract 3. carnival 4. rude 5. shape 6. piece 7. woof 8. wool 9. wagon 10. gal **E.** 1. bear 2. fir 3. fare 4. pear 5. hair 6. wear 7. ore 8. fore **Page 41: F.** Across: 3. purse 4. harm 6. or 7. girl 8. rare 9. more 10. herd; Down: 1. tear 2. hare 3. pare 4. horse 5. mark 6. germ **G.** 1. harp 2. fort 3. air 4. verb 5. forty 6. park 7. tar

## LESSON 13

**Page 42: A. oi/oy:** foil, coy, loin, oink, soy, join, toy; **ou/ow:** sour, tout, wow, down, fowl, round, jowl, count **B.** 1. loud 2. soil 3. toil 4. bout 5. gown 6. our **C.** 1. mouse 2. gown 3. oil **Page 43: D.** 1. e 2. h 3. i 4. c 5. g 6. a 7. d 8. j 9. f 10. b **E.** 1. no 2. yes 3. yes 4. yes 5. yes 6. no **F.** Sentences will vary. **Page 44: G.** 1. toil 2. sour 3. joy 4. loud 5. now 6. down 7. town 8. boy **H.** 1. hour 2. foul 3. oil 4. soy 5. owl 6. town 7. joint 8. bow 9. toy 10. mouse

## LESSON 14

**Page 45: A.** 1. boom 2. hoot 3. fool 4. tool 5. goof 6. loop **B.** 1. hook 2. moose 3. roof **C.** /o͞o/ in loom: noon, ooze, fool, soon, zoom, loose; /o͝o/ in took: good, wood, foot, cook, nook, look **Page 46: D.** 1. school 2. Zoom 3. mood 4. noon 5. zoo 6. book 7. hood 8. goose **E.** Possible: 1. baby 2. thunder 3. fife 4. cow 5. ghost 6. owl **F.** 1. no 2. yes 3. yes 4. yes 5. yes 6. yes **Page 47: G.** 1. also 2. chilly 3. peek 4. fine 5. seep 6. midday 7. chef 8. lumber **H.** 1. book 2. root 3. pool 4. zoo 5. goose 6. boot 7. loom 8. moon 9. soot 10. moose

## LESSON 15

**Page 48: A.** 1. jaunt 2. haul 3. paw 4. tall 5. halt 6. caw **B. aw:** gawk, yawn, bawl, lawn; **au:** autumn, haunt, cause, fault; **al/all:** call, talk, all, hall **C.** 1. fawn 2. wall 3. vault **Page 49: D.** 1. taught 2. lawn 3. yawn 4. mall 5. tall 6. sauce **E.** 1. caught 2. taught **F.** 1. paws 2. haul 3. cause 4. mall 5. bawl 6. awl **Page 50: G.** 1. tall 2. gaunt 3. halt 4. salt 5. dawn 6. bawl 7. raw 8. fall **H.** 1. wall 2. gauze 3. lawn 4. hawk 5. fawn 6. sauce 7. jaw 8. law 9. pawn 10. ball

## LESSON 16

**Page 51: A.** 1. trap 2. bread 3. prop 4. gray 5. grave 6. frame 7. drip 8. brake **B.** 1. creed, crew, crab 2. freeze, frown, fright 3. drip, droop, drain **C.** 1. groom 2. tray 3. prize **Page 52: D.** 1. fight 2. cut 3. creep 4. pull 5. smile 6. gust 7. jab 8. dull 9. weak 10. path **E.** 1. grow 2. drive 3. draw 4. break **F.** Sentences will vary but should have at least three blend words in them. **Page 53: G.** 1. gr 2. br 3. cr 4. pr 5. tr 6. dr **H.** 1. trout 2. grape 3. frame 4. green 5. drape 6. crane 7. crow 8. price 9. crib 10. brook

## LESSON 17

**Page 54: A.** 1. scale 2. sweep 3. stir 4. score 5. sport 6. smear 7. snap 8. snob **B.** 1. stake, stoop, stout, store, stow 2. span, spore, spout, spare, spar **C.** 1. snail 2. scarf 3. ski **Page 55: D.** 1. scab, sky, smart, sneak, space, stone 2. stain, stalk, steam, step, storm, stub **E.** 1. speak 2. speed, 3. swim 4. spin **F.** Sentences will vary but should have at least three blends. **Page 56: G.** 1. sw 2. st 3. sk 4. sp 5. sm 6. sc **H.** 1. scale 2. skate 3. spoon 4. swan 6. smoke 6. snake 7. skin 8. skirt 9. snow 10. stage

## LESSON 18

**Page 57: A.** 1. blob 2. gloat 3. club 4. play 5. flame 6. slight 7. bloom 8. fleet **B.** 1. blood, blare, blight 2. clad, clue, clean 3. plum, plug, plot **C.** 1. flag 2. plow 3. globe **Page 58: D.** 1. flu 2. plain 3. blew 4. flea **E.** 1. open 2. fast 3. cloudy 4. sad 5. wake 6. work 7. wither 8. sink 9. ceiling 10. curved **F.** Sentences will vary but should have at least three blends. **Page 59: G.** 1. bl 2. pl 3. cl 4. pl 5. bl 6. cl **H.** 1. blob 2. sled 3. glue 4. claw 5. flour 6. plum 7. cloak 8. clam 9. blue 10. blood

## LESSON 19

**Page 60: A.** 1. scram 2. splat 3. split 4. spry 5. strand 6. stroke 7. sprout 8. strain **B.** 1. squad 2. throne 3. strides 4. scrawl 5. threw 6. spray **C.** 1. thread 2. squid 3. screen **Page 61: D.** 1. scrape 2. street 3. throw 4. squirt 5. squad 6. scream 7. split 8. squirm 9. spry 10. stray **E.** 1. scrap, splice, spread, squeeze, strip, threw 2. strap, streak, stripe, stroke, strum **F.** Sentences will vary but should include at least three blends. **Page 62: G.** 1. spr 2. squ 3. str 4. thr 5. str 6. str **H.** 1. screen 2. spruce 3. thread 4. squeak 5. stream 6. scrap 7. throat 8. strike 9. throne 10. straw

**LESSON 20**

**Page 63: A.** 1. pact 2. boast 3. cold 4. lamp 5. find
6. raft 7. hint 8. gasp **B.** Possible: 1. sink, wink, pink
2. best, test, nest 3. hint, lint, mint 4. fold, cold, hold
5. lamp, ramp, damp **C.** 1. nest 2. tent 3. bald
**Page 64: D.** 1. built 2. sank 3. bent 4. found 5. told
6. lent 7. held 8. sold 9. went 10. felt **E.** 1. opinion
2. start 3. lose 4. right 5. hard 6. hot 7. worst 8. slow
9. pepper 10. east **F.** Possible: 1. yes 2. yes 3. no
4. yes 5. yes 6. no **Page 65: G.** 1. st 2. mp 3. nk 4. nd
**H.** 1. mast 2. dusk 3. hand 4. rent 5. mask 6. honk
7. cent 8. rust 9. kilt 10. raft

**LESSON 21**

**Page 66: A.** grass, toss, sorry, bubble, bottle, jazz,
summer, huff, wall, pull, puddle, happy, jelly, furry,
pretty **B.** Possible: 1. dress, less, press 2. fell, well, sell
3. cuff, muff, puff 4. bill, hill, mill **C.** 1. bell 2. rattle
3. gull **Page 67: D.** 1. ball 2. berry 3. cell 4. roll 5. hall
**E.** Possible: 1. snake 2. cat 3. bee 4. soda **F.** 1. pebble
2. buggy 3. grass 4. little 5. battle 6. dinner 7. pill
8. sniff 9. scuff 10. hurry **Page 68: G.** 1. fall 2. tall
3. holly 4. hello 5. yellow 6. pillow **H.** 1. kettle 2. rabbit
3. apple 4. kitty 5. lass 6. ladder 7. cuff 8. doll 9. bull
10. sill

**LESSON 22**

**Page 69: A.** 1. chat 2. shake 3. shave 4. phony
5. chip 6. shore 7. sheep 8. chase 9. chow 10. ship
**B.** Possible: 1. bunch, munch, punch 2. reach, teach,
peach 3. lash, bash, sash **C.** 1. shoe 2. photo 3. cheese
**Page 70: D.** 1. teach 2. push 3. sharp 4. chubby
5. fresh 6. shut 7. rich 8. chill 9. she 10. champ
**E.** 1. chew 2. cheap 3. beech 4. shoe 5. shone
**F.** Sentences will vary, but should include at least
three digraphs. **Page 71: G.** 1. munch 2. cheese
3. peach 4. lunch 5. fish 6. punch 7. bunch **H.** 1. shade
2. graph 3. sheet 4. trash 5. chin 6. wish 7. cheer
8. cash 9. inch 10. shin

**LESSON 23**

**Page 72: A.** 1. thaw 2. sang 3. hung 4. thank 5. path
6. whip **B.** 4. fourth 5. fifth 6. sixth 7. seventh 8. eighth
9. ninth 10. tenth **C.** 1. moth 2. teeth
3. wing **Page 73: D.** 1. hung 2. flung 3. sang 4. swung
5. brought 6. clung **E.** 1. rough 2. witch 3. their
4. whale 5. wear 6. weather 7. ring 8. whine 9. whole
10. while **F.** 1. gh 2. ng 3. th 4. gh 5. ng 6. th **Page 74:**
**G.** 1. mother 2. author 3. father 4. brother 5. thief
**H.** 1. prong 2. laugh 3. thirty 4. song 5. wheat
6. spring 7. king 8. math 9. north 10. hangar

**LESSON 24**

**Page 75: A.** 1. kneel 2. wriggle 3. numb 4. ghost
5. knew 6. could **B.** 1. h 2. l 3. l 4. l 5. p 6. g 7. k 8. b
9. h 10. h **C.** 1. lamb 2. knit 3. wreath **Page 76:**
**D.** 1. wrote 2. wrung 3. knew **E.** 1. night 2. knead
3. wrap 4. plum 5. hour 6. wood 7. knot 8. no 9. gnu
**F.** 1. grind 2. branch 3. still 4. anger 5. rap 6. bite
**Page 77: G.** 1. wrist 2. climb 3. kneel 4. wreck 5. numb
6. talk **H.** 1. wrench 2. crumb 3. comb 4. calf 5. knee
6. wren 7. half 8. knife 9. gnat 10. sign